ACKNOWLEDGEMENTS

I want to thank God for to write this book. I am most and wisdom to recover from growing up fatherless and providing me this format to share the life lessons that I've learned. I know He placed a relationship book inside of me over ten years ago and He kept the desire to write this book alive in me.

To my teachers, Ms. Alma Davis, Dr. Daryl Hobbs, the late Dr. Judy Wells, and the late Ernest Davidson, Jr., your words of encouragement still motivate me to work hard and do my very best. To my girlfriends thanks for all the laughter and tears over the years as we've shared our own dating stories.

To my husband, Cleo, thanks for working hard so I can stay-at-home and raise our sons and understanding my need to write this book. To my sons, Cleo II and Carson, thank you for allowing mommy to take a break and focus on my research.

To my editors, Helen Bungert, and Dr. Stephanie Dunn, thank you so much for your patience and taking me on as a client.

Contents

INTRODUCTION

Daddy's Little Girl: Growing Up Fatherless 4

Chapter 1

My Journey 14

Chapter 2

Looking for Daddy 29

Chapter 3

Shadows of Our Fathers 45

Chapter 4

Dating Without a Daddy 72

Chapter 5

The Dating Challenge 82

Chapter 6

Images of Our Fathers 99

Chapter 7

How Will I Know If He's Worthy of Me? 105

Chapter 8

He's not *the one* if 126

Chapter 9

DATING PREP 101 155

Chapter 10

Dating: A Fact Finding Expedition 165

Chapter 11

His Network 174

Chapter 12

Moving Forward..200

INTRODUCTION
Daddy's Little Girl: Growing Up Fatherless

All throughout my childhood to young adult life, I had this recurring fantasy. I'm maybe ten or eleven and suddenly my real father finds me. He's been looking for me for years and when he actually sees me, he's so overcome with joy he's crying and calling me his baby girl. He sweeps me up in his strong arms – of course he's tall and TV handsome – and he spins me around and I laugh so hard and am so happy that I cry too. I know then that I will be safe, happy, protected and loved. This fantasy never came true.

There's a lot of public discourse about how fatherlessness negatively impacts a child's emotional and social well-being. There's also much discussion about the significant number of fathers who don't pay child support, which means some children suffer economically and live in poverty. And yet, while these issues are well-known and freely discussed in our culture, there is a distinct lack of intensive, ongoing public dialogue about how fatherlessness specifically impacts male-female romantic relationships. One of the keys to this exploration is a neglected dimension–how fatherlessness impacts women. How a woman feels about herself is greatly influenced by how she was treated by her father, or whether or not he was absent or a positive presence in her life growing up. Dr. Northup states, "A girl's father and his attitudes about women create an indelible imprint upon her psyche about her own worth and also about what to expect from a man. If he is warm, loving, and attentive, then she's apt to choose a man who is similar. If, on the other hand, her father is cold, distant, abusive, or possessive, this will also influence a daughter."[1] Research shows females without father figures often become desperate for male attention.[2] I believe women who aggressively seek male companionship attract men who devalue them. My beliefs were further substantiated by a close male friend who said, "Men can sniff out desperate women." I agree!

---

[1] Fathers, Daughters, and Dating
http://www.drnorthrup.com/womenshealth/healthcenter/topic_details.php?topic_id=80.
[2] Grimm-Wassil, C. (1994). Where's Daddy: How Divorced, Single and Widowed Mothers Can Provide What's Missing When Dad's Missing. Woodstock, N.Y.: Overlook Press.

WHAT YOU NEED TO KNOW

Fatherless women may be more prone to falling into various dating pitfalls than their well-fathered counterparts. We may marry without noticing and listening to major signs about our partners, only to later discover our husband's lack of vital relationship skills or capacity to be a loving, mature life partner. Too often, the situation is aggravated by a troubling reality; we haven't dealt with our father-daughter issues and bring that problem into our love relationships. It's not a stretch to suggest that fatherlessness could be a huge contributing factor to that alarming 50% U.S. divorce rate! This means that women need even stronger, clearer dating strategies that empower us to make wise dating and marrying choices.

Because I've been one of those fatherless daughters dating blindly, I know that dating without a daddy is challenging for many women. Growing up without a dad in the home or consistently in my life, I wasn't exposed to a positive image of a strong man. When it came time for me to date and select a mate, I was clueless about what qualities to look for; the picture in my head was at best murky and informed by popular culture rather than personal knowledge. I had to make my own judgment calls about what behavior was acceptable and unacceptable. With no male figures playing a major role in my life, I wasn't well-equipped for the often tortuous world of dating. I had a few big dating breakers, for example, physical or overt verbal abuse, but I suffered from low self-esteem having felt the pain of missing a father who was emotionally and most often physically absent most of my young life. Actually, by the time I had come along, fatherlessness was already sort of a family tradition.

Both my mother and maternal grandmother grew up without their fathers, making them two of the three generations of fatherless women that I'm aware of. Theirs was due to failed marriages. By the time I was a teenager, I identified the lack of stable marriages in my family as causing a legacy of absentee fathers. From my perspective, this was a blemish, a public sign that the women in my family were doomed to being single women and lacked some vital skills or knowledge necessary to sustain romantic relationships and marriages. I believed this family background somehow diminished my value as a potential wife. No one ever countered the message. Failed relationships with men became a self-fulfilling prophecy for me, but I didn't want to pass this on to the next generation. I prayed for an intervention.

My prayers were answered when I went to college or so I thought at the time. I began to study and gain some understanding of the plight of fatherlessness while majoring in sociology. I read about how this lack negatively impacts the social and emotional development of children and ultimately influences human behavior and decision-making, especially romantic relationships. What became clear during my studies is how impactful fatherlessness is even on the social and cognitive development of children.

For some time research has suggested the negative impact fatherlessness has on children. In his book, *Life Without Father*, David Popenoe states, *"Growing up without a father may be a root cause of many social ills—from crime to academic failure."* Some of the issues which can be associated with fatherlessness are juvenile delinquency, drug and alcohol abuse, teenage pregnancy, welfare dependency, and child poverty, all can be directly traced to fathers' lack of involvement in their children's lives.

The cognitive perspective is the area of psychology that focuses on mental processes such as memory, thinking, problem-solving, language and decision-making (Weiten, 2008).[3] The evidence indicates that economic hardship, high levels of anxiety, and low parental involvement are critical factors for the causation of poor cognitive performance in children without fathers (Shinn, 1978).[4] Researchers have also identified a strong correlation between a father's nurturance and a child's IQ. Based on this theory, psychologists also feel that lack of healthy interaction may hamper cognitive development (Shinn, 1978),[5] which may lead to academic problems such as low grades or becoming a high school dropout.

What some children experience early in life obviously influences their adult reasoning, social conditioning, and life choices since childhood encompasses the socialization process. Girls learn how to be daughters, sisters, wives and mothers. Boys learn how to be sons,

---

[3] Weiten, W. (2008). Psychology: Themes and Variations. (7th Ed.). Belmont, CA: Wadsworth.
[4] Shinn, M. (1978). Father absence and children's cognitive development. *Psychological Bulletin,* 85(2), 295-324.
[5] Ibid.

brothers, husbands and fathers. However, if there is no male in the home, little boys may not become familiar with the roles of husband and father and little girls with the roles of wife and mother; even if a family adheres to a nontraditional value system regarding these roles, this is where children get a template for their future adult behavior and attitudes towards the opposite sex and love relationships.

Given my identity as a black woman from a family of single, fatherless black women, I was especially interested in the distinct impact of fatherlessness on African-American girls and women. Like so many of my peers, I received little preparation and training about what I should seek and expect from a life mate. I never saw my mother in the role of a spouse or glimpsed a positive love relationship that she had with my father or someone else. My only experience of her is as a single mother. I didn't have any knowledge of a functional two-parent home except for what I saw on the tail end of my adolescence from *The Cosby Show*, movies, and the occasional rare associate that had that unusual family situation. Still, the sociological perspective provided incredible insight into relationships and the human motivations behind decisions and why people feel the way they do. What I loved about sociology is that it offered practical solutions to real life problems. It offered a general understanding of a specific population or social problem from a distance. Unfortunately, it took more years and a lot of dating mishaps before I was able to effectively incorporate this useful sociological knowledge into my actual choices and behavior. Having been baptized through study, my professional life, and serious trial and error and arrived at a place of peace and personal relationship fulfillment, I offer this book as a useful tool for all of my fatherless sisters. *Dating Without A Daddy* is more than an analysis of the problem and a laundry list of don'ts. I offer the 'must do's for avoiding being a victim of fatherlessness and for successfully discovering a worthy life partner. Consider this an intervention for those of you who don't have a father or father figure to tell you some of the things you need to discern in the men you pursue and the men who pursue you.

I use not only my dating experiences but those of a number of women to highlight the dating choice errors that fatherless women are vulnerable to, as well as offer a practical guide to offsetting these and conducting wiser decision making in the dating process. The relationship stories here have been collected over the years and represent a population of women who are mostly educated, single, and never married, including many of the African-American women I have known as friends, professional acquaintances and women I met along my journey who wanted to share their stories; their names have been changed to protect identities. A few are divorced women with children. The most striking commonality with these women is that most were successful professionally but dismally unsuccessful in forging healthy romantic relationships. My intention is not to bash men because that would serve no purpose.

For those of you re-entering the dating scene after a long-term relationship has ended (death, divorce, mutual agreement), consider this book a useful guide for you as well. If you are a very young woman, this book is a conversation that I wish I had at sixteen. For others, even if you did grow up with a father in the home, he may have been an emotionally distant figure who felt uncomfortable discussing male-female relationships with his daughter. This book sheds some light on what your father couldn't or didn't articulate to you. As an African-American sociologist, I feel obligated to share what I know about relationships with my African-American sisters. However, what I've realized over the years and even more so while writing this book, is that regardless of age, race, status or income, many single women have a commonality – our desire for a man who is a good human being with positive qualities with whom we can entrust our love, strength, vulnerability, and future.

Chapter 1
My Journey

My childhood was similar to that of many women. I grew up in a single female-headed household. My parents divorced and my mother was responsible for raising three daughters. Unfortunately, when my parents separated, my father abandoned his daughters too. I don't know why some men do this, but they do. The reasons are never good enough to justify to a child why a father would subsequently choose not to maintain his responsibility. At least my father paid child support, but I needed so much more than money – emotional support, affection, and guidance. Although he lived in close proximity to us after the divorce, seeing him was a rare treat. I would see dad out and about in the community; sometimes he would blow his car horn at me and keep driving. At the time, it didn't register in my young mind as a sign of disrespect, but it did wound me deeply every time this distant, random act occurred. Wasn't his own daughter lovable and important enough for more than a toot of his horn? Why did he avoid real interaction with me? In later years, I concluded that he hadn't intended any harm. Like so many men, he didn't understand his value as a father to his children but as a young girl I felt like some anonymous neighborhood girl to my own father. I sure didn't feel like his daughter. I internalized his behavior as a benchmark of what treatment to expect from men.

The toot of my father's car horn was an apt metaphor for the level of his involvement in our lives. He spent time with us only occasionally; it was never on a consistent basis. Dad, as I called him, never spent any holidays or our birthdays with us. However, he did attend all graduations from high school and college, but throughout my childhood and adolescence when I was forming opinions about my future husband, my father wasn't available, and I didn't feel comfortable having relationship talks with my mom.

Since I was so conscious of my mother's failed relationship and that of her mother's as well as other women in our family, her advice wasn't really credible. My mother didn't appear to be confident in her judgment of men. She did give me some broad hints. My partner should be a nice Christian man with a steady job. That was the sum of the advice. She didn't go into great detail or explain what specific characteristics should be encompassed within this general mandate. I made a lot of assumptions about men since I had just sporadic up-close interaction with only a few distant male relatives. The most specific trait that I associated with Mr. Right or a 'good man' was his ability to maintain a roof over my head and put food in my mouth. I didn't have any male in my life to dispute this notion. By age sixteen, with a few sketchy clues from my mother, I jumped to the front lines of dating. I was a lost, would-be daddy's little girl, on her way to being grown up and looking for love. I looked for it in wrong faces and places.

I dated Howard, my first love, for a few months. Howard was three years older than me and already out of high school. One weekend afternoon, Howard dropped me off at home and went to meet his friends to play basketball. We had plans to hang out later that evening. I sat at home waiting for him, but he never called or came by. As my curfew approached, I knew my mom wouldn't let me go out with him. I turned on the television to watch the local news; there was a mug shot of Howard and two of his friends. They had been arrested for a string of robberies in a nearby neighborhood. Over the next few days, reports surfaced about the backgrounds of the men who committed the robberies. This is how I learned that Howard was actually older than he'd said and a high school dropout with a criminal record. Needless to say, my mother banned me from seeing him.

    I was so hurt and embarrassed by Howard's actions. My friends teased me for going with a thief. Everywhere I went, people asked me about him. I avoided telephone calls and stopped spending time with friends, but I couldn't escape it. I felt foolish for dating a criminal. Why hadn't I noticed his continuous excuses for why I had only met his mother and siblings in passing, or demanded details about his actual job, and the steps he was actually taking towards his future? I certainly had never thought about asking him whether or not he'd been in any trouble with the police or ever engaged in criminal behavior. I just assumed that Howard was a good guy based on what he told me. On top of that, I felt abandoned and unworthy, the same feelings that my non-relationship with my father invoked. Still, I was too uninformed and naïve to transform my approach to guys and dating. My romantic adventures over the next few decades weren't much better. I went out with a decent guy or two, but at the time I didn't recognize them as such. One of these good men would later become my husband. I dated more men who were toxic. I exemplified how poorly fathered daughters can begin bad dating habits and choices early in life that can become a pattern until and unless the problem is clearly recognized and addressed.

> *A stable and nurturing childhood is essential for the healthy psycho-emotional and spiritual development of a human being. While we may understand what is supposed to happen to us physically, we must begin to better understand what happens to children mentally, emotionally and spiritually as a result of the families into which they are born. My father did not have the required understanding.*
>
> *For most of my life, I believed that my father had broken many of my bones. They were emotional and psychological bones; things no one could see, things that caused me to limp through life clutching for and holding on to people and situations that often rendered me immobile. He broke my heart by leaving me in the care of his mentally unstable, violently abusive mother after my mother, his first mistress, had died. He broke my trust by ignoring the wounds on my body and terror in my eyes when he would return after a long absence, asking nothing about the bruises and wounds on my body. He destroyed my innocence by exposing me to his many lovers who were nice to me because they wanted to be with him. He broke my sense of value and worth with his critical, analytical assessments of what was wrong with me and how I needed to work harder to fix myself. Worst of all was his refusal, inability or unwillingness to show me even the slightest sign of affection. My father never kissed me, hugged me or told me that he loved me. As my only living parent, he*

became the filter through which I saw myself, the possibilities for my life, the world and all men.[6]
—*Iyanla Vanzant*

Iyanla's negative experience with her father may have contributed to her becoming a teen mom and being twice divorced. I paid for 'dating without a daddy,' that is not having a real, loving relationship with my father and not dealing with the pain it caused. If there was a major social defect that a man could possess (financially and socially inept, married, attached to mama, unemployed, drug and/or alcohol addicted, unmotivated, dishonest, unfaithful, etc.), I attracted it! These men shouldn't have been dating. They should have been in therapy working on their issues; more importantly, I should have been doing the same instead of dating. This is why dating is challenging and why I was so confused about what a quality guy and appropriate life partner might look like. I still didn't know some basic facts such as how statistics indicated that I would more than likely date men who came from a single-parent home. Additionally, children

---

[6] Vanzant, I. (2010). How to Get Through What You're Going Through: Who's Your Daddy? Huffington Post. http://www.huffingtonpost.com/iyanla-vanzant/how-to-get-through-what-y_1_b_787832.html.

from single-parent homes were more likely to face negative life outcomes.

Boys from homes without a father are more likely to be aggressive, experience academic and social failure,[7] become incarcerated,[8] be a teen father,[9] and/or abuse substances.[10] I wasn't interested in dating men from this background. Knowing this information would have suggested that I also needed to interrogate from where the men I dated drew their image of manhood, a girlfriend, wife, and husband, and by extension, how they perceived and treated women. For instance, was his idea of a man distorted and coming from gangster movies? I never thought to question whether or not his conditioning came from a negative role model in his life or whether or not his mother had been primarily responsible for the care of her children which he then would expect from his wife. Had he witnessed

---

[7] http://www.ncoff.gse.upenn.edu/content/brief-father-presence-matters-review-literature.
[8] Harper, C.C., & McLanaham, S. (2004). Fathers Absence and Youth Incarceration. *Journal of Research on Adolescence*, 14 (3), 369-397.
[9] *Teachman, Jay D. (2004).* The Childhood Living Arrangements of Children and the Characteristics of Their Marriages. *Journal of Family Issues 25, 86-111.*
[10] Survey Links Teen Drug Use, Relationship With Father. *Alcoholism & Drug Abuse Weekly 6 September 1999: 5.*

his mother tolerating abuse from men? Did he see his mother and father go to work every day or just one of them, and was the other parent the kind who sat at home without contributing much to the quality of family life? I started searching for a husband, but wasn't taking the time to examine how a man might function in that role. In addition to not understanding that I needed to ask more questions and probe further into a man's background and character, I tended to fall prey to a number of other pitfalls. When it comes to fatherless women and relationships, Gabriella Kortsch states, "Perhaps the arena in which the most painful process of learning how to deal with the early lack of a father is played out is in that of relationships. If a girl has not been assured of her value as a woman by that early relationship with the father, she finds it difficult to relate to men precisely because she may often unconsciously seek to find that recognition in the eyes of the beloved…and this may lead her down an early path of promiscuity... which in turn makes her feel she is 'bad,' but on she marches, relentlessly visiting bed after bed, locking in a fierce embrace with man after man, in the hope that this one or that one, or the next one will finally give her that which she never had as a child –

validation of herself for herself. Other women may choose another route, falling in love with an older man and thus marrying 'daddy.' Another possible scenario (and there are many more which for reasons of space can not be touched upon in this article) is that of avoiding relationships totally, or of avoiding the engagement of one's emotions."[11]

One of the worst of these was my tendency to overstay my welcome in a clearly unhealthy relationship; I dated obviously unsuitable guys for too long. I was like that big original Jennifer Holiday hit, "And I'm Telling You I'm Not Going." Only my life wasn't a Broadway play and the reality didn't play as well as the song. A hundred different signs might be shouting that I should leave the guy alone, but I'd cling on, accepting nonsense, determined to achieve the love and companionship and romance that I craved. Staying too long led me to give my own power to the men I dated and give them

---

[11] Kortsch, G. Fatherless Women: What Happens to the Adult Woman who was Raised Without her Father? http://www.trans4mind.com/web2printer/print.php.

permission to treat me badly. Since I didn't feel worthy of a good guy, I accepted what I received too much and ended up being gutted emotionally, physically and mentally.

It got so bad that I was terrified that if I continued getting into negative relationships, I wouldn't be emotionally fit enough when a decent man came along. I had been called a "bitch," had money stolen out of my wallet, been physically threatened [a guy threw an object at me], been cheated on and lied to, and yet I stayed. I was stupid. I invested a lot of time and money in men I really didn't respect and believe in. It's difficult to have a high opinion of someone who treats you badly. My dating experiences ultimately got so negative that I removed myself from the dating scene for a while. The decision to stop dating was hard because by then I was nearing my mid-30s and my biological clock was just ticking away. I wanted to marry and have children. However, I had to get off that bad-dating treadmill. If I wanted to date suitable men, I had to identify what I was doing wrong. I had to recognize that I didn't have the basic tools to get a good man. I had to deconstruct myself and my relationship patterns by asking myself, "What's wrong with me?" There I was, a respectably raised African-

American Christian woman, highly educated, financially independent, child-free, humorous, and fairly attractive to the opposite sex, and yet I was in dating hell. I had to understand why I was dating all of the wrong men.

I sat myself down and wrote out my experiences with the men I had dated and contemplated what lessons I could draw from these relationships. I pondered this for months. One day I was talking to one of my best friends who came from a two-parent home, and she described the man in her life and how he was a solid, stable man. He's "just like my dad!" she said. Eureka! In that moment, I finally realized that I didn't have my daddy as a gauge to compare men to; my dad hadn't been emotionally available to me or there to give guidance and support as I entered the world of dating. I was also bitter that my father was alive and healthy but wasn't around for me. That's why I continuously dated the wrong weak men!

I was trying to fill a void in my life and replace my dad. I was seeking approval and acceptance from men I dated because I didn't receive it from my dad. If a man loved me that would mean there was nothing wrong with me. I was seeking validation for being a woman and for just being a human being worthy of love. I wanted someone to confirm that I was decent, attractive, smart, and appealing. I needed a man to validate that my educational and financial accomplishments made me worthy of a 'good' man and lifetime commitment. Most importantly, I wanted a man to tell me that he could love me in spite of my weaknesses. I know that a lot of you can relate to this. I hadn't been clear about these daddy-related issues, so I was failing in trying to forge a healthy love relationship and eventually marriage with a man. It is as lifestyle expert Iyanla Vanzant says, "In order to make self-supportive choices and effective decisions and to make productive actions, you must have a well-ordered mind."[12] Though I was a woman raised in a Christian environment, I hadn't taken to heart the familiar, useful biblical scripture that Vanzant echoes and which I'd heard in church more than once: *For God has not given us the spirit of fear; but of power, and of love, and of a sound mind.* 2 Timothy 1:7.

---

[12] Vanzant, I. (2008). Tapping the Power Within: A Path to Self-Empowerment for Women. Smiley Books. United States.

This realization empowered me to confront my father. I gave him a piece of my mind about how his absence, non-interest, and lack of demonstrated affection towards me had impacted my life. I demanded answers, an explanation, for his choice in removing himself from fathering my sisters and me. He couldn't articulate one, but he apologized. I forgave him; we cried, and I began to heal, and move forward. I was in my mid-thirties. My resentment receded. I no longer chose to have my emotional energy consumed by that pain. My relationship with dad grew stronger after this encounter. I asked him many questions about his family, relationships, and life in general and he answered them. For the first time, my dad became a real part of my life and a vital part of the positive social network that I saw I had to build with good, platonic guy friends and female friends who had healthy romantic relationships and marriages. One of the male friends I sought dating advice from would eventually become my husband. Now, I talk to my dad almost daily about the challenges of life. He shares his life lessons, which are invaluable, with me.

After a year or so, I started dating again and got the first test of my growth – Pastor Jeff White. When I first met him, Pastor White told me that he was divorced and had custody of his young son and daughter. We went out to dinner and the movies a few times, and he admitted to having two additional children by different women. That was a major red flag, but I was still a work in progress. There came a point when we were trying to decide what to do on our next date and the Pastor offered an interesting proposition. He said, "I would like to take you to a cheap hotel, where we can play cards, talk and watch movies." I remember thinking, *I don't do cheap hotels. I haven't played card games since I was a child, and we can talk in person or on the telephone*. Like I said, I was still a work in progress. I should have run and never looked back right then.

Still, the old me would have automatically naively entertained Pastor White's invitation to spend an evening with him at a hotel. Why? I didn't want him not to like me. And according to him, he was looking for a wife. I wanted to be considered. The new me, however, interrogated his proposition closely and even consulted with my stronger, wiser network of intimates. I called my father and shared the proposition. Dad said, "Baby, never go out with a man who won't take you to his home; he may be hiding something or someone." I consulted with a few other friends in my network. They agreed with my dad. I wished that my dad's advice had been with me when I first started dating because I had gone out with men and never visited their homes. Once a regular dating relationship was established, I always invited the guy to my place because I felt more comfortable entertaining in my own setting. My father's advice was better late than never. I rejected the Pastor's proposition and him. My old self might have invested months, maybe even a couple of years in him, but my new wiser self spent only about six weeks with him. Months later I ran into a former classmate of mine who knew Pastor White. He confirmed that the Pastor had a First Lady already. He and his wife had been married for several years. The whole experience confirmed that beginning to resolve my daddy issues, as well as having a loving father-daughter relationship, could play a major role in my dating life.

Chapter 2
Looking for Daddy

My dating choices reflected my childhood family. I moved forward with relationships without taking the time to evaluate why my previous relationships had failed. Take a moment and reflect. How was your childhood relationship with your father? Was he loving and attentive or did he discount you? Have you ever asked yourself what sets you apart from some women who find healthy, loving romantic relationships? Analyze your dating and romantic relationships. Write down the romantic relationships you've had and identify problems. See any patterns? Relationships end, of course, for a host of reasons, not all of them bad. However, notice the tendencies in your dating choices and the issues that emerged. Do you choose men who are incompatible with your lifestyle, personality, and your relationship needs? Are the men you tend to be attracted to repeatedly socially, emotionally, and/or financially dysfunctional? Have you chosen to become involved with men who engage in irresponsible drug and/or alcohol use or who demonstrate other destructive and violent behavior? Are the men you've dated controlling, dishonest, unfaithful or emotionally disengaged? Try to articulate your responsibility in the dating and relationship choices that you've made. Next, in just a sentence or two, try to articulate your feelings about how the absence of your father or troubled relationship with your father has impacted your sense of self and your life. Do you see connections between your relationship choices and that impact?

It took decades for me to come to the realization that the root cause of many of my relationships problems could be linked to my father. My father's absence caused me to seek to replace the void he left in my life through the men I dated, regardless of flaws that should not have been overlooked. I remember desperately wanting my father to be my dad and a part of my life. But an overwhelming majority of my childhood friends, both male and female, were living without their fathers as well. Statistics indicate that seven out of ten African-American children are being raised without a father.[13] By the time I reached college, fatherless daughters were in the process of becoming

---

[13] http://datacenter.kidscount.org/data/acrossstates/Rankings.aspx?ind=107

the new normal in our culture and a social phenomenon that posed serious problems.

DATING WITH & WITHOUT DADDY

Daddy is a term of endearment that signifies an affectionate, consistent relationship between a father and child. "Any fool can be a Father, but it takes a real man to be a Daddy!!" —Philip Whitmore Sr. Little girls who are so blessed love being a beloved daddy's girl, those not so blessed secretly crave to be one, as I did. Unfortunately, for too many young girls, particularly a disproportionate number of African-Americans, it is just a fantasy. "When one has not had a good father, one must create one." —Friedrich Nietzsche

For many of us who didn't have a dad, as we transitioned into womanhood, there became this constant need to fill this gap with any male figure. I know this story quite well. Fatherless women become especially vulnerable to dating in the dark, often times looking at only a man's physical traits and personality rather than focusing on his character and relationship skills. Ideally, the most appropriate and best training ground I know to obtain sound knowledge about romantic relationships is by witnessing a stable two-parent functioning home. This is where children can readily learn how a husband and wife should love and respect each other and interact in a committed relationship. This is also perhaps the best way for females to see what qualities they should seek in men they're dating.

    Even daughters whose fathers were missing, or unable to be fully active in their daughters' lives because of death or illness, can suffer from the pain of having not been able to have fulfilling relationships with their fathers. Although death is not controllable, a daughter would still likely miss this bonding. A father who is absent from his daughter's life by his own choice potentially causes further trauma to his daughter's psyche. 'Absentee father' primarily refers to fathers who willfully did not parent their daughters. I've talked to women who have fathers that died, fathers addicted to alcohol or drugs, fathers who are incarcerated, and fathers whose identities they didn't even know. Regardless of the circumstances for his absence, a child can feel rejected. Absentee fathers have no or inconsistent contact with their children and have little influence in their children's upbringing, value systems, and social lives. From my perspective, a man who pays child support, but has no emotional or physical involvement in your life, is still an absentee dad. The most dedicated and loving single-parent female head of the house, like my own mother, cannot always provide their daughters with sufficient information on how to detect a quality man or fill the possible void left in their children by the absence of their father.

In a single-parent household, information about relationships may unfortunately be limited. Girls often get culturally socialized into a general set of dating rules as I did within the church and African-American community in which I came of age. The don'ts included, don't be promiscuous, don't wear too much make-up, don't wear revealing clothes, and the do's included cautions such as pick a man who can take care of you [financially that is], find a man who goes to church, be with a man who loves and respect his mother and so on. In 1970, a majority of children grew up in two-parent homes, but by now there's a taken-for-granted trend of children being raised by mostly moms.[14] As a sociologist and as the daughter of divorced parents raised

---

[14] Kreider, R. and Ellis, R. (2009). Living Arrangements of Children: 2009. *Current Population Reports.* Issued June 2011.

in a single-female headed household within a community dominated by the same, I know that one of the most significant social issues of our times is the increasing numbers of fatherless children, due to rising divorce rates, a high number of out-of-wedlock births, too early parenthood, and other socio-economic factors. Though there is now a generation of professional women who choose to become parents without partners because they don't want to marry, or their dreams of love and marriage have not panned out, there are even more who grow up fatherless due to unfortunate circumstances [broken relationships, divorce, etc.]. Children missing fathers is a universal epidemic which crosses racial and ethnic lines, income and educational status and age groups. Every child is vulnerable.

The failure of manhood in America -- fatherhood -- has reached epidemic proportions. And unless our religious and cultural institutions say enough is enough, we are going to see another generation of children growing up with dad absent and unaccounted for. It's time for men to man up, so children can grow up with an equal amount of love and affection from both parents. [15]— Roland Martin

---

[15] Martin, R. (2009). Commentary: Man up and be a real dad
2009http://fatherhood.about.com/gi/o.htm?zi=1/XJ&zTi=1&sdn=fatherhood&cdn=parenting&tm=57&gps=248_8_1024_651&f=11&su=p284.13.342.ip_p504.6.342.ip_&tt=3&bt=0&bts=0&zu=http%3A//www.cnn.com/2009/POLITICS/05/06/martin.fathers/index.html.

Addressing a congregation at one of Chicago's large black churches, "Too many fathers are M.I.A, too many fathers are AWOL, missing from too many lives and too many homes," Mr. Obama said, to a chorus of approving murmurs from the audience. "They have abandoned their responsibilities, acting like boys instead of men. And the foundations of our families are weaker because of it."[16] These words were spoken from then Senator Obama. When elected into office, President Obama created Fatherhood Initiative's *Fatherhood Buzz*--a pilot outreach initiative designed to disseminate information about responsible fatherhood and parenting.[17]

This demographic shift from two-parent to single-parent homes has unfortunately resulted in fathers being increasingly more distant or absent from their children's lives on a day-to-day basis, though certainly there are fathers who are the heads of households and raising their sons and daughters full-time. Yet, there are approximately 24 million children who don't know what it means

---

[16] http://www.nytimes.com/2008/06/16/us/politics/15cnd-obama.html.
[17] http://www.whitehouse.gov/sites/default/files/docs/fatherhood_report_6.13.12_final.pdf.

to have a father.[18] Fatherlessness has become one of the most destructive demographic trends that we've seen in recent times because its ramifications are far-reaching and helping to change how couples experience and define relationships.[19]

For example, a recent Pew Survey indicates that 40 percent of people believe marriage is obsolete. One explanation for the results of this study is that fatherless children may have a different mindset about traditional marriage. Without dad, children are more likely to suffer from a host of psychological and social problems.[20] A father's absence in his children's lives ultimately can produce deficiencies such as insecurity, low self-esteem,[21] and a sense of shame and hopelessness.[22] Even into adulthood these shortcomings cloud judgment, particularly for women pursuing romantic relationships as research suggests.

---

[18] U. S Census Bureau 2009. Dulton Adult.
[19] Blankenhorn, D. (1996). Fatherless America: Confronting Our Most Urgent Social Problem. New York. NY. Basic Books.
[20] Rosenberg, J., & Wilcox, B. (2006). Office on Child Abuse and Neglect, U.S. Children's Bureau. The Importance of Fathers in the Healthy Development of Children.
http://www.childwelfare.gov/pubs/usermanuals/fatherhood/.
[21] Griffin, D. (1998). Fatherless women. Milligan Books. Los Angeles, California.
[22] Erickson, B. (1998). Longing For Dad: Father Loss And Its Impact. Health Communications, Inc. Deerfield Beach, Florida.

Academy Award winner, actress Halle Berry, has been very successful in her career but has two failed marriages, to baseball player David Justice and singer Eric Benet.

> *I wish I had known then that I was not the marrying kind. It would have saved me a lot of time, heartache and grief over the years. I made all the wrong choices when it came to love. I have been an idiot. But, now, it is like a gift to myself seeing more clearly and making better decisions. One thing was unavoidable. My father left us when I was young and that did affect my life. If I had a good father in my life, growing up, then I do not think I would have made the mistakes I made. I would not have been lost in love. I would have had a good role model and known what to look for. As it is, I had to find out about marriage from the men I've married. I have done it twice and I am not going to do it again. The traditional form of marriage is not for me.*[23] — Halle Berry

Some women don't believe that they need a man to help raise their children. It isn't, of course, that many women haven't or don't raise sons and daughters successfully alone. However, fatherhood encompasses more than the act of supplying sperm for procreation. Paternal figures and members of the opposite sex add value to

---

[23] http://www.thesun.co.uk/sol/homepage/woman/3519775/Halle-Berry-Growing-older-is-no-big-deal-even-in-Hollywood.html.

children's lives. Single mothers can raise children who are morally sound, smart, capable, and all-around good human beings. I know plenty of successful men and women who didn't have a dad in the home. As a matter of fact, I'm one of them. My mother raised daughters who hold degrees and achieved professional positions in the corporate world. Academically, I accomplished what only one percent of the population has, that is, a doctorate degree.[24] Yet, I suffered emotionally from the loss of my father and failed miserably when it came time to pursue my own love choices. I didn't have a clue about the dating process!

The research suggests the benefits of fathering on the lives of children. Studies show that fatherless children are more likely to commit crimes, abuse alcohol or drugs, be depressed, suicidal,[25] end up incarcerated,[26] drop out of high school[27] and suffer emotional

---

[24] Educational Attainment 2000: Census 2000 Brief. Issued August 2003. http://www.census.gov/prod/2003pubs/c2kbr-24.pdf.
[25] David, P. (1997). Life Without A Father: Fatherhood And Motherhood In A Diverse And Changing World. A Paper Presented At The Annual Conference of the NCFR.
[26] Harper, C.C., & McLanaham, S. (2004). Fathers Absence and Youth Incarceration. *Journal of Research on Adolescence,* 14 (3), 369-397.
[27] U.S. Department of Health and Human Services. National Center for Health Statistics. Survey on Child Health. Washington, DC; GPO, 1993.

problems.[28] Adolescent girls raised in households without fathers are far more likely to engage in promiscuous sexual activity and get pregnant early out of wedlock.[29] Single mothers too often have to assume the roles of both mother and father simultaneously. Mom is the breadwinner, nurturer, provider, and disciplinarian. Further, she must act as the primary source of domestic socialization for her children. For little girls and boys who grow up in this environment it's hard to distinguish the parental roles because they are witness to mom being a one-woman show. They often don't get the opportunity to observe two people negotiating daily household responsibilities and finances, sharing, and communicating. Research shows that children who grow up in single-parent homes are more likely to divorce than children from intact homes.[30]

Being rejected by daddy or missing a father's affection and guidance can create a sense of worthlessness. This becomes the unfortunate foundation upon which too many women build their dating

---

[28] Remez, L (1992). Children Who Don't Live With Both Parents Face Behavioral Problems, *Family Planning Perspectives*. January/February 1992.
[29] Mattox, W. (1999). The Role of Fathers in the lives of Their Daughters.
[30] Wolfinger, N. (2005). Understanding the Divorce Cycle: the Children of Divorce in Their Own Marriages. Cambridge University Press.

and relationship patterns. Who we attract reflects where we are in our lives or rather within ourselves. This is why it's unhealthy to date when you have unresolved wounds, feel lonely, and are desperately seeking love. It's not that motherless daughters don't experience some of the same issues in finding love. Similarly to fatherless daughters, motherless daughters may also feel a void that they end up seeking to fill. However, my focus is on fatherless daughters because absentee fathers are more pervasive in our society and of course because this is a crucial part of my story.

Children without fathers, like children from other household backgrounds, grow into young men and women who are expected to fulfill social roles such as mom, dad, husband, and wife. Because a significant number of children are growing up without their fathers, a great many may be ill equipped to meet these social expectations. Both men and women are dating with insufficient information on how to fill their social roles. It's not easy being a spouse or parent or partner in a committed relationship; most of what we absorb about these roles comes from the environment we're raised in, unless we undertake the work of learning new ways of thinking about them and occupying them.

Dating requires wisdom and discernment. In the old days, more daughters were likely to get some of this from the dad taking on the responsibility of teaching their daughters through their experiences as men who've dated and married. For instance, a close friend of mine, Gina, is married to Jesse, and they have a teenage daughter, named Leanne. Since Leanne could walk and talk, Jesse has always taken her out on monthly dates. He shows Leanne what she should expect from men. He opens doors, holds her hand, and pays the bill. He doesn't want his daughter to accept any behavior from a man that is less than what he has shown her. From my perspective, Leanne will probably have healthy dating experiences.

A father's loss becomes problematic for dating women in at least two significant ways: (1) they lack clarity about the best qualities upon which to build healthy relationships and what to seek and expect in the men they date and (2) they set unrealistic expectations about what to expect from the men they date and marry. Hence, when women missing daddies date, there are frequently two outcomes – clinging to unhealthy men when the relationship has long expired and/or engaging in a series of dead-end relationships they don't fully invest in, for fear of rejection or abandonment.

> *You can accept or reject the way you are treated by other people, but until you heal the wounds of your past, you will continue to bleed. You can bandage the bleeding with food, with alcohol, with drugs, with work, with cigarettes, with sex, but eventually, it will all ooze through and stain your life. You must find the strength to open the wounds, stick your hands inside, pull out the core of the pain that is holding you in your past, the memories, and make peace with them.*[31]
> — *Iyanla Vanzant*

The differing ways that two young college women assessed a man that each dated provides a telling illustration of the above. Michelle and Amy both dated Ryan, a popular guy on campus. Ryan was a nice-looking guy in the most popular fraternity. Michelle, who grew up in a two-parent home with an attentive father, was smart and very attractive. Michelle dated Ryan for only a couple of weeks before deciding to stop dating him when she noted that he had anger problems. She felt that Ryan had the propensity to become violent. Michelle's father had been a devoted family man who treated Michelle and her mother with respect and care. When Amy found out Ryan was

---

[31] VanZant, Iyanla. (2001). Yesterday, I Cried: Celebrating the Lessons of Living and Loving. New York. New York. Fireside. Simon & Schuster.

available, she honed in on him and swooped him up. Amy, also an attractive, academically smart young woman, was a social butterfly. She was also a daughter who grew up with a father who chose not to participate in her upbringing. Soon after Amy began dating Ryan, he showed signs of the anger that had turned Michelle off. Initially, she delicately tried to speak with him about it, but she continued to date him. Within six months, her disposition changed. She withdrew from her friends who noted how sad she seemed. She and Ryan dated for several years until Ryan broke up with her because he found someone else. Amy was devastated.

Quite possibly, the big difference between how the women handled themselves with Ryan had to do a lot with their paternal backgrounds. Michelle reaped the benefits of having a positive father in her life. Amy accepted behavior that Michelle took as a warning of Ryan's unfitness as a romantic partner and potential life-mate. Amy didn't feel empowered and confident enough to reject Ryan as an unworthy partner. This is not to say that women with fathers don't make poor choices, because they do. I interviewed women who come from intact homes but have dated foolishly as well. They also divorce, have children out of wedlock, and date dysfunctional men. However, women who have strong ties with good dads tend to be less likely to invest a lot of time with men whom they detect have major flaws and men who don't exhibit the positive behaviors and character modeled by their fathers. They are more likely to identify the warning signs. It's hard to identify a man of integrity if you don't know what he looks like or haven't been exposed to him! My point is that it's harder to seek what you don't know or haven't witnessed.

Chapter 3
Shadows of Our Fathers

A woman's relationship with her father is very fragile and sensitive. Any breach made by dad can easily break his daughter's heart. A daughter depends on her dad for protection and guidance. A dad's rejection can cause serious life-long problems since it will undoubtedly affect a woman's self-perception. Multiple violations such as broken promises, abandonment, verbally or physically violent behavior, or emotional detachment can have irreversible damage on a young girl's psychological development. The father-daughter bond is the spark that fuels all future romantic relationships for women. A daughter's perception of her father is based on interaction (i.e., does he spend quality time with her), and perception how she views (his integrity, trustworthiness, respectability, leadership, compassion, etc.).[32] By the time a girl reaches her early teens, she has enough information and exposure to her father to have subconsciously

---

[32] Grimm-Wassil, C. (1994). Where's Daddy: How Divorced, Single And Widowed Mothers Can Provide What's Missing When Dad's Missing. Woodstock, N.Y.: Overlook Press.

formulated a perception of him and other men based on what he models in his roles as husband or partner and father.

DADDY LOVE

A biological father contributes to your genetic heritage via sperm donation. You may have his skin tone or the color of his eyes or the shape of his lips. You may also find his name on your birth certificate. Sometimes, the biological father is not the one who becomes 'Dad' or 'Daddy' – the guy who undertakes the responsibilities of fathering, including the economic, physical, social, emotional, and financial demands. I use 'Daddy' or 'Dad' to signify the intimate bonding and paternal love and care that comes with an ideal father-daughter relationship. Dads are men who do the daily grind of participating in their children's lives by fulfilling their responsibilities. According to Horn, Blakenhorn and Pearlstein (1999) in the book, "The Fatherhood Movement: A Call to Action," fathers fill a wide variety of roles in their children's lives. However, I believe there are six essential roles men must provide for their daughters. Dad's role encompasses some of the following primary tasks: (1) manifest essential moral and social traits and establish a religious or spiritual foundation [or a belief system for living]; (2) financially provide and teach a strong work ethic; and (3) provide love, protection, and validation of their children's self-worth. Dad's performance in these core areas sets the tone for their daughters' [as well as sons'] perception of male-female relationships. Fathers serve a key fourth dual function: giving their daughters a sense of security as well as empowerment while providing useful guidance about appropriate and inappropriate male behavior, and helping them figure out safe boundaries as they embark upon dating and falling in love. A dad's success or failure in fathering helps to shape how his daughter will receive and give love to other men.

MORAL VALUES & SPIRITUALITY

According to a report by the Pew Forum on Religion and Public Life, a majority of people in the United States profess Christianity, specifically the Protestant religion. If a family practices the Christian faith, then dads play a pivotal function as a guide into the spiritual or religious foundation of their daughters' lives. This is important since the religious belief system generally encompasses rules or lessons about marriage, courtship, sex, and moral individual behavior. If you grew up in Christianity, the church may be one of the main places where you developed your thinking about how husbands and wives should treat each other and about who may or not be an appropriate choice. In my case, the mantra that I should look for a mate who could provide for me was bolstered by popular scriptures that I read and heard growing up in our church: "But if anyone does not take care of his relatives, especially the members of his own family, he has denied the faith and is worse than an unbeliever" (1 Timothy 5-8) and "Whoever refuses to work is not allowed to eat" (2 Thessalonians 3-10). If you grow up observing prayer and worship as a major facet of your father's and family's lives and your parents' relationship with each other, then this is likely to become a yardstick by which you will choose the men you date and commit to. Certainly, children might learn about prayer and worship and the lessons outlined from their religious institution from mothers as I did. Yet, the other major impression on me in this regard came as a result of seeing a few fathers who took their families to church faithfully and served active roles within the church. These men were regarded as good men;

sometimes, I would study them during church service, especially as they soothed, rocked, or quietly disciplined their little girls.

PROVIDE FOOD, CLOTHING AND SHELTER

According to the Christian ethic in which I was raised, fathers should have a work ethic motivated by their desire to take care of not only themselves but their family. In the twenty-first century, more women work and choose to do so than in my early years. Gender roles have changed as more fathers often take on the primary role of home caregiver while his wife or girlfriend is the primary breadwinner. This should be decided between two mature partners based on the needs of the family and mutual decision; however, there are several ways in which it is problematic if a woman ends up with the sole financial responsibility of taking care of the couple. If the situation results because of the man's lack of skills, work background, or interest in providing and contributing and/or he is not taking on the responsibility of caring for the family's home and children, then this is a poor foundation for a long-term commitment. Further, even if he is home by mutual choice because he is deemed the most suitable for taking care of the children and home, a woman needs to choose a mate who has a good work ethic and training, or the education to be self-supporting and support a family. What happens if your career takes an unexpected detour, and he needs to assume financial responsibility for the family or at least begin contributing? Growing up witnessing examples of men in church who work and provide for their families certainly made an impression on me; I valued what grown folks applauded as a "working man." It goes without saying too that even if a father does not live with his children, he should be financially supporting them along with assuming other parental responsibilities. I knew that my father faithfully financially assisted my mom with meeting the costs of raising us, and at least in that way, I respected him. A girl who grows up not seeing her father as well as other men in her universe take on financial responsibility for their children may cause her to undervalue this important function. She may end up selecting partners who don't value this responsibility or she may end up overvaluing it, placing a man's money and professional status over his character.

OFFER LOVE, PROTECTION, & VALIDATION

Children obviously need the love and emotional support of both parents. This helps build confidence and a sense of security. Good dads and moms desire to protect their children from harm and make them feel safe and secure. Both girls and boys may view their dad as a hero. Little boys may want to be 'just like daddy;' girls may want to marry men who are 'just like dad.'

> *Fathers are far more than just 'second adults' in the home. Involved fathers–especially biological fathers–bring positive benefits to their children that no other person is as likely to bring. They provide protection and economic support and male role models. They have a parenting style that is significantly different from that of mother, and that difference is important in healthy child development.*[33]
> —*David Popenoe, Sociologist, Rutgers University*

Before my parents' divorce, when I was a little girl, I remember playing outside with a young boy named David. He pushed me off of my bike and started riding it. I asked for my bike and he refused. I didn't

---

[33] Building Blocks for Father: Building Block 1: Appreciating How Fathers Give Children a Head Start (2004). U.S Department of Health and Human Services Administration for Children and Families Administration of Children, Youth and Families Head Start Bureau.

cry though because I knew that when I went to get dad, he would get my bike back. Daddy was big and strong; he could do anything and no harm would come to him. To this day, I remember telling David, "I'm going to tell my daddy." And that's exactly what I did. I ran into the house and told my daddy what David did to me. Dad came outside and diffused the situation; David returned my bike and apologized.

Daddy was my hero. When my parents separated, my safety net was gone and I felt all alone. Although I was blessed to have my mom, I didn't see her as a hero. I saw her as needing protection too. From that point on, I tried to resolve my own issues and only went to mom with my problems in extreme situations. Without dad, my ultimate hero was gone.

Each sex has unique needs that dads fulfill differently as well. Girls benefit from their dad's validation in that if a father conveys to his daughter that she is worthy of love, affection, and respect early on and exemplifies this in his treatment of her and his wife, then the daughter will be more likely to view this as the gold standard by which to judge men. Consistent validation from her father will help to give her self-confidence to seek healthy relationships. The beautiful thing about great dads is that they view their daughters in terms of their beauty and potential, reaffirming these in verbal as well as non-verbal interaction: "you're so pretty," "look at your beautiful smile," "princess," and "you are so smart, you can be anything you want to be." Hearing such words over and over again builds self-confidence and self-esteem, and over a period of time a girl has the foundation to grow into a woman who believes this to be true. Desiring protection may cause fatherless daughters to crave paternal protection and seek to fill this need through the wrong love choices. Nia Long states, "I didn't have much of a relationship with my father growing up and I'm sure I thought that didn't affect my romantic relationships, but now I know it did." Now, she explains, "My father and I are in such a good place." Nia continues, "Our relationship has helped me deal with some of my relationship stuff. I'm calmer, less clingy and demanding."[34]

DATING GUIDANCE & BOUNDARIES

There are many benefits that come from having a responsible dad. It provides young girls with a safe male model and allows them to

---

[34] Essence Magazine August 2012.

experience what it feels like to be valued by men.[35] While growing up with such a dad, a girl picks up important clues about appropriate behavior both as a social being and a woman. Dad, along with mom, imposes rules and/or offers firm responses if his daughter behaves or dresses in ways contradictory to her age, identity, and upbringing. Though he may be nervous about his daughter being old enough to date and later to marry, a good dad wants his daughter to attract quality men. A father's constant emotional engagement in the life of his daughter helps to shape her perception of love. A dad's affirmation of a daughter's femininity is instrumental to womanhood and the ability to love.[36]

A healthy father-daughter relationship is a girl's first experience at receiving unconditional love from the opposite sex. She receives caring with no strings attached. A daughter doesn't have to give up anything to please him. Being her daddy's daughter is enough. Her success in life and happiness is his reward. It is dad's responsibility to assist in empowering his daughter through knowledge about men so she

---

[35] Erickson, B. (1998). Longing For Dad: Father Loss And Its Impact. Health Communications, Inc. Deerfield Beach, Florida.
[36] Ibid.

can differentiate between who might be right and wrong for her. His constant teachings and his love by example can give daughters wisdom and discernment in the dating process. When a girl brings her first love home, dad is the guy that often gives his honest opinion of him or regards him with healthy suspicion. When she has issues in her romantic relationships, dad may provide a much needed insight into the dynamics at play within the problem. This is a healthy part of developing positive dating patterns. Strong dads are involved in their daughter's lives consistently. Of course, it's ideal when a father resides in the home with his children, but consistent involvement in his children's lives, whether he lives nearby or far away, is just as essential. He has an integral role in his children's lives by giving them love, guidance, and support.

A father may likely interrogate any man that you bring home. He feels that it is his responsibility to help eliminate men who are not good for his daughter. If a relationship fails, dad is there to wipe away his girl's tears and tell her that the right guy is still to come. Since fatherless daughters don't have a connection to dad, they may find themselves more readily involved with men who prey upon vulnerable women. It's said that women are attracted to men like their fathers, and that's not surprising. In an interview, Peggy Drexler PhD, the author of "Our Fathers, Ourselves: Daughters, Fathers, and the Changing American Family" (2011) states, "Some women were treated with respect -- even gallantry -- by their fathers, and they demanded nothing less from the other men in their lives. Conversely, some were treated with insensitivity, or even emotional cruelty. And their attitude is: 'Been there. Won't do it again.' Sadly, there were those who followed the classic assumption that women will seek to repeat what they experienced growing up. It's not a universal truism, but it certainly does happen."[37]

TIES THAT DON'T BIND

I've learned over the years that fatherless women sometimes place dad on a pedestal that he hasn't earned. I was a part of this group too. Before I move further, it's important for you to take an objective look at the relationship you had with your father as a young girl. Sometimes girls with absentee fathers create a fantasy image of him to

---

[37] http://www.self.com/health/blogs/healthyself/2011/05/did-you-marry-your-dad.html.

help cope with the pain of his loss. This fictional picture of him is very soothing in the moment but is problematic in the long run. Be honest about the kind of father you really had/have especially while reading this section. Was he a strong dad who was actively involved in your life on a regular basis, both financially and emotionally, or a weak one who chose to have irregular, little, or no interaction with you and no financial and/or emotional support?

HE'S NOT THERE FOR YOU

Men who have weak ties to their daughters are likely to have had little involvement in their daughters' lives or be dysfunctional fathers who harm instead of love, protect, and nurture their daughters. A dad that lives outside the home and rarely spends time with his children and sporadically or never calls or seeks interaction with his children is not likely to establish a strong father-daughter foundation. The same is true if a father doesn't consistently acknowledge special events in his children's lives, interact with his children's friends, attend parent-teacher conferences, and participate in the daily, weekly decision-making that parenting demands. When it comes to parenting, a weak father may not be concerned about fulfilling his societal roles and responsibilities or only doing so on a limited basis for appearance's sake or on the rare occasion that it isn't inconvenient. He may live by his own creed which may not necessarily fall within your expectations of a father. A man may have a weak paternal instinct or may be too disinterested, self-absorbed, and/or not emotionally mature and compassionate enough to be committed to relationships which need to be nurtured, developed and maintained. Fatherless daughters may suffer from growing up with this kind of behavior. This is just one explanation of why romantic relationships for fatherless daughters are challenging and often times produce negative results.

This was certainly the case with a young woman I encountered named Lori whose only significant contact with her dad was his annual summer family reunion. He would call her mother a few weeks before the trip to confirm her attendance. They would spend two nights and three days together, and she was elated to spend this time with him. This, unfortunately, was the only real time and interaction she got with him. Lori wished they could spend more time together and expressed this to him. However, outside of his annual family event, he rarely communicated with his daughter; she was lucky if he called her around her birthday and during the Christmas season. She would reach out to her father, but he rarely responded.

Though it is disturbing, there are biological fathers whose financial support is needed but they are not doing so and not even ashamed of not providing for their children. Too many sons and daughters grow up witnessing their mothers' struggles to take care of the family. These challenges may not cause him to be concerned. Children sometimes retain an amazing regard for bad parents, both mothers and fathers who fail to be there for them in multiple ways. However, it is difficult for children not to grow old enough to perceive this failure in the face of the willful absence of the parent. A dad who has strong ties to his daughter is just the opposite of what I have just described. Females who have strong relationships with their dad may try to date men who are equal to him. If dad works hard to provide for his family then his daughter may be more inclined to date men who have a work ethic. If dad expresses love by being affectionate and holding hands, his daughter may be drawn to a man who demonstrates the same. Women that did not have a consistent, healthy model of fatherhood and manhood in their fathers often, like I did, fill in the gaps about their dads with fantasies. If no other male in their lives steps up to serve as a loving, consistent father figure to her, then a fatherless daughter may have no needed model, no frame of reference for identifying a suitable mate, which puts her at risk to make poor dating choices. Dating in the shadow of paternal absence sets up many of us for bad dating syndrome characterized by a few major symptoms, some of which I've already mentioned.

LOW SELF-ESTEEM

I'll never forget Katie who suffered from low self-esteem. She was very self-conscious about being overweight and didn't feel good about herself. She didn't think men found her attractive and felt uncomfortable in the presence of men. Katie had been rejected by her father when she was a young girl. When she grew up, she still wanted validation from him and decided to reach out to him again. Her father finally embraced having her in his life. They were just becoming reacquainted when Katie's father died suddenly. She never got the acceptance she wanted from him. She had always hoped to have a relationship with him and now that would never happen. Katie was surprised to learn he left her a small inheritance. She assumed this was his way of making up for abandoning her, but Katie wasn't concerned about the money. She wanted her dad.

She fell into a deep, deep depression and isolated herself from family and friends. After her work days, she went home, ate, took to her bed and slept or chatted online. Over the course of a few short months, she gained more weight and hated how she looked, so she decided to date online. This provided a safe barrier. Her strategy was to allow a man to fall in love with her personality before seeing her in person. Katie met a really nice guy named Doug online. He lived several hours away in another state. Doug shared his misfortunes with her. Since he was open about his life, Katie felt comfortable chatting with him about her situation. She told him that she had been abandoned by her father when she was a little girl and had recently gotten in contact with him before he died. She even told him about the inheritance. Katie told Doug she was lonely, confused and felt unattractive because of her weight gain. He told Katie what she longed to hear from a man. He assured her that she was smart, confident, and beautiful regardless of her size. They talked on the telephone, exchanged cards and even wrote letters to each other. Katie began to fall in love with Doug. She invited him to her home, and he was happy to oblige. She prepared a candlelight dinner for Doug. When she opened the door and heard his voice, she fell into his arms crying. Finally, here was the man who understood her pain and loved her. They talked for a while and sat down for dinner. They ate and the last thing Katie remembered was sipping on a glass of wine.

She woke up disoriented, with a headache, trying to remember what had happened. She yelled for Doug. No response. She hoped that whoever had done this to her, hadn't hurt Doug. She tried to get out of bed. She was tied to the bedpost. Katie had been raped. She lay there screaming for help for hours. She knew her neighbors were at work but hoped someone might hear her. Finally, a neighbor did and called the police. The police rescued her but Doug wasn't there. She had been robbed. The few photos she had of her dad, heirlooms from her grandparents, jewelry, cash, checkbooks, her wallet and a few paintings – all of it was gone. Even though the officer told her that Doug was the likely suspect, Katie didn't want to believe it. She gave them the little information she possessed about Doug, including his letters. She didn't even know what kind of car he drove. The officers said that she should be grateful to be alive. They also thought that he hadn't pulled off the crime alone. She found out a few days later that neither Doug's name nor address was valid. Katie was devastated and didn't feel safe in her home or community. Her case was never solved.

FEAR OF BEING ALONE

Carol's parents divorced when she was a toddler. Her father remarried, moved out of state, and had additional children. Carol spoke to her dad just a few times a year. By the time she was in her early 20s, she was the mother of two children by her high school sweetheart, Craig. They broke up a few years later and Craig disappeared from his children's lives. Carol was terrified that she would end up raising her children alone. She began dating Kevin, and after just a few short months together, she became pregnant. Kevin already had a child he couldn't take care of. He encouraged Carol to have an abortion, but she refused. Kevin broke up with her. She was hurt and became depressed; she hated being alone. She grew up without a father and desperately wanted a dad for her unborn child and her other children. Carol begged Kevin to come back to her and promised to do whatever she needed to do in order to make him happy. Even though Kevin was unemployed and didn't have a steady income, Carol let him move in. He supported her by going to some prenatal visits, and he was even in the delivery room for the birth of their son. Carol now had a father for all of her children. However, whenever she spoke to Kevin about finding a job, he evaded the discussion. A few months after their child's birth, Kevin confided in Carol that he hadn't finished high school and any job he obtained would be low paying. Therefore, he had a little side hustle – selling drugs. Carol was terrified. She was a professional woman who owned a legitimate small business. She never envisioned herself dating a drug dealer. Still, she didn't want to press Kevin and make him leave her.

One night, Carol put her children to bed and laid the baby in his crib. She and Kevin began watching a movie. Suddenly there were gunshots. They fell to the floor, Carol crawling towards the children. Thankfully, no one was injured. When the police arrived they took statements and ran their names in a criminal database. There was a felony warrant out for Kevin; the police took him into custody. It took all of that for Carol to deal with the daddy abandonment issues that had led her to place an unfit man over the welfare of her children and herself.

FEAR OF BEING ABANDONED

Often, women who feel abandoned by their fathers fall into bad love choices. They migrate to men who are as emotionally, socially, and physically unavailable to them as their fathers might have been. They crave security and love but select men who are predestined to do what they fear the most – abandon them. Men such as Kevin fall into this category and so do married men. If you are one of these women, you should understand something very important. Though many single women end up dating married men whom they hope will leave their wives and commit to them, marriage with a man from an affair has over a 75% chance of failing.[38] Rummaging through another woman's home seeking her husband should not be considered as a dating option. There are many reasons why marriages borne out of an affair don't last.

---

[38] Hein, H. (2000). Sexual Detours: Infidelity And Intimacy At A Crossroads. St. Martins Press. New York. NY.

Couples who participate in these relationships don't generally get to know each other through dating well enough to determine whether or not they are compatible. Such couples function in secrecy and shame; social outings are limited. A married man can't take his mistress to his home church and openly worship with her and chances are, if you are that mistress, you can't take him to yours. You also are unlikely to be able to take each other around your respective extended families for the holidays and special events.

In the book, "New Other Woman" (1985), by Laural Richardson, she wrote, "There is a certain amount of prestige involved in being in love, since love is associated with being beautiful and desirable. So, when a woman is in love, she wants to tell the whole world, to shout it from the rooftops. She wants the admiration rightfully due her. But when a woman is in love with somebody else's husband, that feeling is tainted; the whole world is a narrow one, the shout has to be muffled, and the rooftops are barricaded."[39]

---

[39] Richardson, .L. (1985). New Other Woman. The Free Press. A Division of MacMillian, Inc .New York. NY.

When a married man dates outside his marriage, his goal is not to explore compatibility and he is not looking for a life partner. Though men, like women, cheat for different reasons, they primarily want to escape commitments or responsibilities or they're merely interested in fulfilling their sexual appetites. Shelly realized these truths the hard way. An educated, single, professional woman in her late twenties, Shelly desperately longed to be a wife and mother. Her parents divorced before Shelly was five; by the time she was eight, her father had remarried. Shelly barely saw the father she adored. She only interacted with him a few times a year and an occasional awkward phone chat. She fell into a relationship with a successful, married businessman named Daniel, after ending a long-term relationship with a man she had wanted to marry. Daniel promised Shelly he would leave his wife as soon as his seven year old daughter was a little older and more independent. However, Shelly was still pressuring Daniel to leave his wife three years later. Daniel finally told Shelly that he was never going to end his marriage. Shelly was distraught.

Then, Shelly met Matthew at a conference. They were smitten with each other. The problem was that Matthew too was a married man with three small children. Matthew leaned on Shelly and vented about his wife not keeping their home clean, or how she was career driven, and neglected him. Shelly promised Matthew that she would do things differently than his wife. Matthew also promised that they would be together as soon as his children grew a little older. Shelly was hopeful. She had finally found the man of her dreams. They dated and traveled together for several years. Matthew even introduced Shelly to his children, and she even babysat for him on a few occasions. Shelly was confident he would leave his wife for her, but Matthew was torn between his wife and Shelly. Eventually, Matthew decided that it would be in the best interest of his children to remain with his wife and terminated his relationship with Shelly after four years together. She was devastated.

Shelly had invested almost two decades of her reproductive years from early twenties until late thirties in relationships with married men. She went into therapy after one more short relationship with a married man.

SEXUAL PROMISCUITY

Ashley's father was with their family until she was four years old. Her parents' divorce was contentious; her father was so angry and wounded that he only heeded the custody agreement for the first months, which allowed him two weekends a month, summer vacation and a couple of holidays with his daughter. He also had the right to speak with her via phone as they wished. Ashley had been a daddy's girl up until then. For years, she could not understand the separation and could never understand her father's shocking withdrawal from her life. She lost her virginity at fourteen years old – the first time an older boy [three years older] paid her serious attention. By the time she graduated from high school, she had been sexually active with a handful of males.

In college, she was so sexually promiscuous that by her junior year, she lost count of the number of men she had slept with. Ashley had sex with a wide variety of men ranging from students, athletes, professors, administrators, and men who lived in the local community. Ashley equated sex with love. The sexual encounters only filled her desire to feel loved temporarily so she engaged in more sexual activity. However, the fall of her junior year, Ashley decided that she had to slow down and stop going with so many men. She managed to abstain for several months and found that she felt stronger, but she did not realize that she needed to uncover the source of her sexual behavior.

She met Jack that spring semester and fell fast for him. He was a student at a nearby college, and they shared the same career goal to become a lawyer. Within a few weeks, Ashley and Jack started a sexual relationship. She let her guard down and didn't insist on him wearing a condom. In less than three months, Ashley became pregnant. She shared the news with Jack, and he became upset. Jack wasn't ready for a steady girlfriend or to become a father. He thought it was best for them to finish college. He encouraged her to have an abortion. She was devastated and reluctantly agreed. She saw her own mom struggle with having children during her teenage years. Ashley terminated the pregnancy and was an emotional wreck. Her choice to end the pregnancy conflicted with her Christian values, and she fell into a deep depression. Jack couldn't cope with her being sad and ended the relationship. Ashley was left alone to grieve her loss.

Within a couple of months, Ashley began another sexual relationship as she tried to cope with the loss of Jack and her child. One weekend, there were a group of male students from out of state visiting their fraternity chapter on campus. Ashley was attracted to one of the men, Lucas. She invited him back to her place for sex, and he obliged. Since it was a one-night stand, she didn't think to get any contact information from him. Ashley later discovered she was pregnant again. She was in shock. Ashley contacted Lucas through one of his fraternity brothers. When she called him, he didn't recognize her name. He admitted to having sex with another woman the same weekend. Ashley felt humiliated because she had to describe herself to him to jog his memory. He only vaguely remembered her. Lucas told Ashley once the kid was born, if she wanted, they could get a DNA test. She went through her pregnancy alone. At twenty-one, Ashley dropped out of college and moved back home with her mom to become a single mother. She finally went into therapy in her mid-twenties after finishing college while raising her young son.

Chapter 4
Dating Without a Daddy

Unless you live in a society in which marriages are pre-arranged, dating is the primary mode for you to meet a boyfriend and a husband. Dating is rough and in some instances it can be dangerous. It's also not so simple; though it would be nice, a single woman desiring a mate might not grow up with him or meet him in her hometown or be able to rely upon the matchmaking skills of close mutual friends and family. It's great when this is the case since friends and family can confirm or provide knowledge about the man's character, integrity, work ethic, religious beliefs, family values, and background. However, globalization and technological advances have changed all of this. You have to get into the trenches and uncover information on your own. It's easy not to have any information on a guy. He can fabricate almost anything, and you wouldn't even know it. If you come with baggage from unresolved father issues and especially suffer from the pain of not having had your father's presence in your life, then you must be particularly careful about avoiding becoming a victim when you date. One of my most painful memories was being a man's 'cover girl.' My 'boyfriend' had boyfriends which he hid from me. Looking back, I see that I made it easy for him to do so. I did not interrogate gaps in information or the contradictory behavior he sometimes exhibited.

FATHERLESS BLACK WOMEN DATING

I was vulnerable not only as a woman wounded by the lack of my father's active participation in my life but as a black woman acutely aware of the father and black male crises within the African-American community. Statistics indicate that about 67% of black children are raised in a single parent home.[40] A majority of black children are being raised by women with no male in the home. This means that there are communities of black children who are rarely witnessing functional black couples. Think about this for a moment. Almost every little girl that I grew up with came from a single-parent home. As a result of the absence of fathers and nuclear black families, many of us became easily indoctrinated in the media's representation of love and marriage for dating and marrying cues. The problem is that the media's portrayal of

---

[40] http://datacenter.kidscount.org/data/acrossstates/Rankings.aspx?ind=107.

men and women dating is often based on superficial qualities such as celebrity good looks and material affluence. I fell for this and applied the media standard of men in my own dating life. It warped my sense of reality when it came to male-female relationships. It took me decades to get a clear and practical definition of what type of men to date. I didn't have any role models in my environment. Therefore, my image of relationships rested upon a combination of qualities I read about in magazines or images of families I saw on television. Secretly too, my image of the perfect mate fit that tall, strong-armed, handsome, brown-skinned dad in my dad fantasy.

My ideal man was a six-foot, chiseled, ebony professional with no prior marriage, no children out of wedlock, and no criminal record. I was looking for a black Ward Cleaver or Mike Brady type of potential father for my children. I also wanted him to be funny and reliable like Cliff Huxtable and enjoy sipping a glass of chardonnay with me and going on long walks hand-in-hand. My expectations weren't real. I never saw Ward or Mike or Cliff Huxtable reviewing a household budget with their wives or handling family issues after the thirty-minute episode ended. I just knew that whatever minor issue cropped up it was over in thirty minutes.

Black women are continuously bombarded with how dismal our dating and marrying prospects are due to a lack of eligible, quality black men. In 2009, a Yale study found 42% of African-American women remain unmarried, compared to only 23% of white women. This statistic was cited by popular social media such as CNN and ABC.[41]

This popular dialogue has a negative psychological effect on black women and has caused some panic and justifiable concern among them. Many black women see black men as a scarce resource. They thus feel compelled to do whatever is necessary in order to end up with their ideal black man, which includes making desperate choices by trying to convert him into someone he's not. I fell into being a desperate black woman who feared I wouldn't find that available, ideal black man and end up childless and alone.

---

[41] http://abcnews.go.com/Nightline/FaceOff/nightline-black-women-single marriage/story?id=10424979#.UcDWqfmcc8k.

There are a reported two million more black women than black men.[42] The reality is that there are not enough functional black men to go around.[43] Due to the lingering effects of discrimination, black men face some of the hardest circumstances in our society. Black men have high rates of unemployment and are more likely to be high school dropouts. The lack of education impacts their ability to provide income for their families. This ultimately impacts the male-female relationships and the black community. Other factors such as black men marrying non-African American women and incarceration contribute as well. Finding a suitable mate can be intensive work, and more so for black women limiting themselves to finding black men who are the image of their fathers, or harder still for black men who will fill the fantasy of the black father they never experienced. I eventually came to realize that it was alright for me to seek partners across racial lines and that there are, despite reports to the contrary, some good, decent, hardworking black men.

---

[42] We the People. Blacks in the United States. Issued August 2005.
[43] Banks, R. (2011). Is Marriage For White People? How the African-American Marriage Decline Affects Everyone. http://www.blackstarnews.com/news/125/ARTICLE/6191/2010-01-01.html.

I was on the dating scene for more than two decades, and it was scary! I had the emotional scars to prove it. However, I found the strength to heal and learn from my experiences. I didn't know it at the time, but I bypassed some decent men, and fell straight into the hands of the perpetrators, men who were merely pretending to have it together. Why? Because in my desperation about my dating chances as a single black woman and in the midst of my unresolved daddy issues, I didn't pay attention to details that I should have, evaluated men by their surface appearance too much, and overlooked good men who possessed the positive traits that I needed. Not knowing how to distinguish between an appropriate and inappropriate man to date caused me to waste almost two decades of my life in dating hell!

DATING WITHOUT DADDY?

Regardless of your racial, ethnic, religious or class background, if you've experienced a break in the father-daughter relationship or never had one and always felt the absence, it's worth asking how your father's absence negatively affected your relationship with men. If you have consistently dated the wrong men then it may be because you are locked in the affects of dating without daddy. Do you have a habit of staying in negative romantic relationships too long? Do you accept married men as options just because you crave love and/or feel lonely? Perhaps you don't feel that you deserve anyone better than men who treat you badly or you've had your heart broken so many times that you no longer trust anyone and you no longer have confidence in your choices. If you're exhausted, and your heart, soul, and sometimes your bank accounts are depleted trying to keep a man so you won't be alone, consider whether you're suffering from dad's absence. As difficult as it may be, begin to address the following questions:

- What is your relationship like with your father?
- Has he explained why he abandoned you? Can you forgive him?
- Do you blame yourself for your father's absence?
- Do you define relationships with men by having sex?
- Do you worry that you are not good enough for some men?
- Do you get in relationships with men and become co-dependent?
- Do you get involved with men who don't/can't commit?
- Do you try to buy material items for a man so that he will love you?
- Do you date multiple men at the same time to avoid commitment?
- Do you fear you have poor judgment in selecting men?
- Do you date men who are emotionally unavailable?
- Do you date men who are incompatible because you fear being alone?

If you have no relationship with your father or it was very dysfunctional, and the answer is yes to one, several, or all of the questions above, you are probably falling into some of the following major dating pitfalls.

CHOOSING LOOKS OVER CHARACTER

I know that other women, like me, have let the media and surface appearance define relationships for them as well. I remember when I was an undergraduate college student and I lived in a co-ed dorm where each resident had her own room. One late evening, I heard one of the girls crying and knocked on her door. Sherry's background was similar to mine. She was raised by a single mom and had little interaction with her father. Sherry and her boyfriend got into a fight; Lewis, the boyfriend, had gotten both verbally and physically abusive. Sherry was extremely upset, and I could tell bruises would appear by morning. Since he had beaten her, I assumed the relationship was over. I told Sherry that she would find a man who loved and respected her. Sherry said they were not breaking up because he was a nice-looking brother with beautiful light eyes, and he had just pledged into a fraternity; she couldn't let him go.

They were still dating on graduation day. I didn't keep in contact with Sherry after college. I just know that regardless of how handsome a man might be, no woman can be happy in a violent relationship. But over the years, I've thought about Sherry and wondered how things would probably have been different if Sherry had been raised with an attentive, loving father or if she had stopped to address her dad issues. Her abusive boyfriend looked ideal because of his handsomeness and social popularity. The media's image of love creates a false sense of security and those of you who seek men based purely on looks and material possessions will only be hurt in the end. I know because I did it.

My definition of love was based too much on looks, feelings and academic accomplishments. If he was nice looking, I would want to go out with him. The more emotions I felt, whether positive or negative, the more I associated that with love. The emotion of love fades over time. Don't get me wrong; you should have feelings for your partner but love is more than that. At one point in time in my life, I thought love was being in pain. The more pain I felt the more in love I thought I was. The major lesson I learned over the years is that he must also treat you well.

I remember choosing looks over character when I dated Joseph. Our childhood backgrounds and academic accomplishments were identical. He was nice looking, educated and smart. That's what attracted me to him, but his words were harsh and sharp. He was bitter and had the propensity to be violent. I will refer to Joseph more later on. I learned that love is an active function and how a man treats you, regardless of the physical package he comes in, is very important. Accept men who may be shorter than your desired height or weight, or may only have a high school diploma. Having a nice looking man is completely irrelevant if you're unhappy and he mistreats you.

Chapter 5
The Dating Challenge

Doing research on the dating experiences of women with absent fathers brought some amazing revelations. One of the most important of these was how many women lack basic dating guidance and strategies for not becoming victims of the emotional and social baggage that growing up with no dad or a positive dad may have created. The fatherless women I interviewed had at best a foggy sense that they even needed to develop some critical dating skills. I know from my lack of preparation that dating women need to acquire some knowledge before we develop committed romantic relationships. Four essential elements are necessary: patience, a sound mind, active participation, and discernment.

PATIENCE

The first dating requirement is patience. In the book "Until Today! Daily Devotions for Spiritual Peace of Mind" (2000), Iyanla Vanzant writes, "Patience is a choice. It is the conscious choice to be reliant on the unceasing movement of life. Patience is an ability. It is the mental ability to remember that once the wheels start turning and the movement has begun, the destination will surely be reached – eventually. Patience is a skill. It is the emotional skill of knowing that what you expect, intend and desire will happen when it needs to happen. Patience is a science. It is a spiritual science of using your mental and emotional skills of creation to such an exacting degree that the outcome is assured at the beginning. It is the science of knowing that what you set in motion with your mind, what you believe in your heart, what you praise in your soul must happen – at just the right time, in the right way."[44]

Patience gives you the ability to wait until situations unfold and reveal themselves. In other words, patience is necessary because if you fall into desperately seeking love or a man or marriage, you won't take the time to be discerning and pay attention to cues and details about potential mates, and you will be much more likely to rush into committing yourself. Making a hasty decision in this area of your life can result in devastating consequences with you ending up being more

---

[44] Iyanla Vanzant (2000). Until Today! Daily Devotions For Spiritual Growth and Peace of Mind. Simon Shuster. New York. New York.

wounded than ever. I'm always amazed at women who meet a man and within a few weeks deem him to be "the one" without even the slightest questioning. And yet, they often lack vital information about the background of 'the one' and/or have only been able to observe him under limited circumstances. Even though it may be looking and feeling good, practicing patience will help you to remember that the first weeks and months of dating, the 'honeymoon' phase or heady first rush of love, typically allows a small glimpse into his life and his fitness for a committed relationship.

Of course, there are exceptions, and stories about love at first sight and quick marriages that went along strongly for years, etc., abound. Setting an arbitrary timeline isn't applicable to every dating situation. However, I strongly recommend dating a man for all four seasons twice. Why? You may discover that after two years of dating, the man you initially thought was the one during the first glorious year of dating is not who you should marry. During the first year of getting to know someone, you are on an emotional high and may potentially ignore warning signs which could lead to problems. I can't tell you how many times women have said, "I didn't know he had a drug problem" or "I would have never gotten involved with him had I known he couldn't keep a job." Men who have hidden agendas are excellent at "impression management." Impression management [is performed at a level of consciousness of how others view us] and by manipulating how others perceive us will ultimately influence how people treat us. They tell you what they want you to know and lie by omission. Smart but vulnerable women miss some shocking personal information:

- Drug addiction and drug selling
- Sexual addiction
- Previous marriages and children
- Mental and physical illness
- Gambling addiction
- Bisexuality and homosexuality
- Criminal background
- History of abuse
- STD'S status
- Bankruptcy, debt, and poor credit history

Patience, I know, may be difficult, particularly when your goal is to marry and have children. Biology obviously affects a woman's ability to bear children, and this window is not indefinite. Studies show women are having babies at later ages. Statistics indicate about 1 out of 12 first births were to women aged 35 years and over compared with 1 out of

100 in 1970.[45] One reason women delay childbearing is to pursue a college degree.[46] We live in a culture where a formal education is rewarded by career opportunities and better income which means a better lifestyle. However, when some women decide they desire children and marriage, by then the biological clock is ticking louder. I fell into this group. I was approaching my mid-thirties when I had a regularly scheduled OBGYN exam. I started to panic when my gynecologist informed me that I had multiple reproductive issues which could negatively impact my fertility. He also told me that my age worked against me. "You need to hurry up," Dr. Jones said, "and get pregnant before it's too late."

When I received this news, I wasn't even dating. The prognosis escalated my search for a man. I went to a nightclub looking for a quality man and met Max. He was in his early 40s and a professional man with a daughter approaching her teen years. He had a lot of

---

[45] Matthews, T. and Hamilton, B. (2009). Delayed Childbearing: More Women Are Having Their First Child Later in Life. NCHS Data Brief. No 21. August 2009. In 2006, about 1 out of 12 first births were to women aged 35 years and over compared with 1 out of 100 in 1970.
[46] Livingston, G . & Cohn, D. (2010). The New Demography of American Motherhood. Pew Research Center.

qualities that were 'red flags,' but I bypassed them. He was possessive, aggressive, and controlling. Max wanted me to report my whereabouts 24 hours a day. Initially, I thought he was concerned about my safety until, he showed up at an event he knew I was attending, uninvited. Max wanted us to go out to dinner but I explained to him that I had purchased one ticket months ago to attend the event alone. Max accused me of having a date though I reassured him that I didn't. I guess he didn't believe me and he decided to attend. There were about 200 people sitting quietly waiting for the host to introduce the guest speaker. I didn't see Max walk in the auditorium; however, he must have noticed me. The room was quiet and Max walked over to my seat and cursed me out. He said I should have asked him to come along. I was embarrassed. I got up and left the event. He continued to call and leave messages on my voice mail. Since he didn't know where I lived yet or my work address, I never returned his calls.

SOUND MIND

Dating wisely requires a sound mind. With a sound mind, you practice patience and more easily avoid allowing physical and emotional intensity to overwhelm good judgment; you can develop reasonable, clear expectations of a man and a relationship, carefully consider and evaluate the cues you get through a man's behavior and words, and make appropriate decisions about engaging yourself in relationships and making commitments. Low self-esteem jeopardizes the ability to have such a sound mind – a not uncommon manifestation in girls who grow up hurting and longing for their fathers. This may be due to the sense of rejection, shame and worthlessness fatherless women can feel from being abandoned by dad and the desire to fill up that missing space. Low self-esteem also puts you at risk for depression. Individuals with low self-esteem are prone to depression because they lack sufficient coping resources, whereas those with high self-esteem are able to cope effectively and consequently avoid spiraling downward into depression.[47] This all, of course, jeopardizes your ability to exercise a sound mind. Research indicates 1 out 8 females will

---

[47] Orth, U., Robins, R., and Meier, L. (2009). Disentangling the Effects of Low Self-Esteem and Stressful Events on Depression: Findings From Three Longitudinal Studies. *Journal of Personality and Social Psychology.* August 2009; 97(2):307-21.http://www.ncbi.nlm.nih.gov/pubmed/19634977.

experience clinical depression as an adult.[48] Depression occurs at twice the rate for women as for men. It can be acute and caused by a sudden traumatic event such as the loss of a loved one or it can be genetic and run in families. It causes mental impairment which means you are weakened emotionally and quite possibly, eventually, physically.

Some men specialize in preying on women who are emotionally vulnerable. Dating in a healthy manner requires you to be at peace with your identity and current single status as well as be hopeful but alert, engaging, and active rather than passive. If you are depressed, emotionally unstable and/or vulnerable, then you will likely be unable to make clear judgments about potential partners. Some of the most undesirable men that I dated were during times when I wasn't emotionally healthy enough to handle dating. There are times when it is best to take a break from the dating scene. My ability to reason and exercise good judgment just wasn't there. I was depressed and out dating. This is a toxic combination for disaster. I was guilty of dating when I shouldn't have been, as the Max fiasco demonstrated.

---

[48] National Institute of Mental Health   http://www.nmha.org/index.cfm?objectid=C7DF952E-1372-4D20-C8A3DDCD5459D07B.

Even if a man comes along during a turbulent time in your life and you think he's the one, take a step back and address your issues by taking care of your physical and emotional health through therapy, spiritual channels, and lifestyle changes. When you have too much going on emotionally, you're not going to be as alert as you need to be. If you're experiencing any of the following issues, consider taking some 'you' time before concentrating on dating:

- You have not made peace with your past
- You have untreated depression
- You are emotionally, financially and/or spiritually broken
- You are hurting from a break-up, including a divorce
- You have unresolved health issues
- You are emotionally connected to another man or currently in a romantic relationship
- You have lost a loved one
- You don't feel good about who you are
- You are battling addictions

This is not intended to be an inclusive list, but it is a capsule of common major circumstances that you should regard as warnings that you are not in the best shape to have a healthy dating life.

ACTIVE PARTICIPATION

For some reason too many women, and this includes many fatherless daughters, disengage during the dating process. Dating requires you to be an active participant. It requires some of the fundamental principles of being a good student in school, including doing homework. You have to be a willing, active, engaged and alert participant who pays attention to verbal and non-verbal cues and who can integrate feedback from others. You can't become content with merely having a man in your life and the potential [you decide] of having that man for a husband. The still sexist orientation of our culture continues to configure men as the more active participant in dating. Men assess women and do the choosing while women get chosen or not. Contemporary dating discussions may encourage women to ask men to dance and out for dates, but they largely fail to teach women to be active participants in dating by engaging in thoughtful or intensive assessment of men.

Consider the case of Candace. Candace and Derek dated for about a year. She met his child on a few occasions but never the baby's mother. She attended a few family gatherings but really didn't communicate with anyone. She sat by herself and watched his family interact rather than interact with them and engage in any meaningful conversations about Derek's upbringing or his character. None of Derek's family members said anything to Candace about Derek. When his family did speak to Candace briefly, they asked about her job and how her family was doing. Though Derek did ask Candace to do other activities with him which included his family, shy Candace declined. Candace had grown up with only her mother who, embarrassed about her single mom status and other family issues, tended to avoid her family. Candace met her father for the first time when she was 15 years old; he didn't keep in contact with her. Candace was hurt. She desperately wanted a relationship with her dad but he wasn't interested. Candace didn't take advantage of being around Derek's family the few times the opportunity presented itself. She would later regret this.

After a year of dating, Derek and Candace married. Candace discovered that Derek had a lot of issues that she hadn't detected while they were dating. He couldn't keep a job. He was in arrears in child support. He was an irresponsible parent, and a poor friend and family member. Candace and Derek divorced in less than a year. Candace was angry and bitter towards everyone around her. She felt that his family should have warned her about Derek. A couple of months after the divorce was final, Candace ran into Derek's sister Donna at the mall. Candace had met her at a family event or two, observed her seemingly good humor and gregarious personality but had never really had an intimate conversation with her. That afternoon, the two women talked and Candace learned more about Derek and his family than she had the whole time they were dating. She learned that his parents were thrilled that someone was going to take care of him because they were tired of helping Derek. Prior to marrying Candace, Derek's parents had loaned him money which he never repaid. He even tried to borrow money from them while married to Candace. A couple of years before meeting Candace, Derek's parents had even allowed their forty year old son to move back home. He ate, slept, and watched television all day long. At times, Derek wasn't even on speaking terms with some of his siblings because he never repaid money that he borrowed from them. He had alienated life-long friends with his irresponsible ways and insensitive attitude. Donna concluded with sharing how the entire family was stunned that Derek met a woman like Candace who would marry him.

If Candace would have become an active participant during family events, chatting, involving herself in family games, asking questions, and paying more attention to how others reacted to him, and she had realized that she needed to be honing in on uncovering certain things about Derek, then she would have detected some of these big issues. Part of the problem is that Candace hadn't realized how much she had ignored the pain of not having her father be a real presence in her life as well as the isolation that was the hallmark of life with her mother. She didn't see that it was her responsibility to do some serious homework on Derek, that is delve under the surface of Derek's words and the seeming pleasantness of those occasional family events. Most family members, especially parents, don't go around saying negative things about their children. Still, if you are around the family and/or social network of a man you're dating, make it a point to absorb details and ask some questions as the opportunity comes along.

DISCERNMENT

The fourth dating essential is discernment. I can't stress this enough! A woman out in the dating world can't merely accept a man's word about his complete identity at face value. In a new relationship, most people want to present their best image. Over time, hopefully two people collect enough information to know if each is indeed what has been represented. Unfortunately, a lot of anxious women focus more on words rather than behavior and real information. Dating well requires verifying some information. If you grew up with lots of blanks about your father, then you may be even more vulnerable to unwittingly falling prey to accepting sketchy details about a man you want to date. However, you can practice being discerning and thus learn to cross reference his words and behavior. If there's a conflict between his behavior and his words, then his behavior will give you a more accurate depiction of who he is. Verification involves proving the truth of the presentation. Think of verification as a normal part of getting to know people before inviting intimate relations and permanent relationships. Confirm truth by listening closely, observing behavior, and asking questions. If he claims to be a good father, he will spend time with his children and place their needs over his own. If he claims to be spiritual, then he will desire to attend church on a regular basis. If he has a close relationship with his mother, you will be able to observe this in both his talk and interaction with her.

Think about this. Very few men would openly admit to being gay or bi-sexual, broke, immature, or insensitive to a heterosexual, mature woman that he's interested in pursuing for whatever reason. Some men may not take a girlfriend home to meet mom until they consider it a serious relationship. You may not meet his mother until you've dated for a year or more. However, if you want to invite him into your family and friend circles at some point then you should want and expect him to want to introduce you to his. When you meet the parents, aunts, siblings, grandparents, and long-time friends, study, observe, and interact with them. Dating takes time and requires you to pay a lot of attention to detail. This is how you learn his character.

> *I've learned that so much of the hurt, heartache and disappointment we experience in love could be avoided if we just paid more attention at the beginning of the relationship. You need to ask lots of questions, look for the warning signs of potential problems, and stay focused on what you're looking for in a partner and what you are trying to avoid.* [49] — *Barbara DeAngelis*

---

[49] http://www.barbaradeangelis.com/advice_compatibility.asp#6.

Becoming more discerning and braver about verifying a man's representation of himself transformed my dating life. I stopped staying in relationships that were going nowhere; I could see and eliminate an unsuitable man after the first few dates. I started paying attention to discrepancies between a man's word and his behavior and heeded warning signs that discomforted me. Warning signs demand attention and further investigation. For instance, if a man is gainfully employed but asks you to pay for everything, this is a red flag. A man who says he has a formal education and a profession, but doesn't have a job or career options that reflect this, it is a serious red flag. Many of you have experienced a contradiction between a man's words and behavior but ignored it when you should not have. He says, 'I love you' or 'I'm committed to you' or 'You are the only woman in my life,' but later on, you find out that he's cheating on you. You think back to the broken promises, last-minute date cancellations and missed engagements, his unexplained mood shifts, and gaps and discrepancies in information and you realize that you should not be surprised. This is not encouragement to be paranoid or distrustful but rather to be wiser and empowered.

Being discerning is an active act of self-protection that can save you from harm and wasting valuable time.

Some areas you can easily verify with a little subtlety. For instance, if he works you can suggest coming to his job to take him to lunch. Make sure he's open about his home and office contact information, not just his cell number. Befriend him on Facebook and take note of his interaction style there. Even if you are a modern woman who doesn't mind going Dutch or treating him, let him pick up the tab for the movies, dinner, and concerts throughout the period you date him – this doesn't mean exclusively. Attend church with him. See how members of the church interact with him; go on work-related social events when invited and notice if there are a number of these but he never invites you. Notice whether or not he mentions you to his family if he claims to care about you, and especially if you're considering dating long term and exclusively. The sum of all of these four dating musts is safer and wiser dating!

Chapter 6
Images of Our Fathers

If you're a woman dating for the purpose of being in a committed monogamous relationship, you need to be consciously aware of some of the diverse dangers that come with dating. For women wounded by absentee fathers, it is especially important to be discerning and identify men with certain vices and issues as unsuitable for dating and long-term relationships. Women dating in contemporary culture cannot approach dating presuming the social and emotional health of the men they are attracted to, and that these men come equipped to provide what they need and desire in a mate. A large number of boys are being raised without a dad and in dysfunctional environments. This has a devastating impact. I'm not saying not to date a fatherless man. Many people have had a problematic childhood family background through no fault of their own, so don't exclude a man solely because he grew up without a father. However, the father-son relationship is just as important as the father-daughter dynamic. If your partner is fatherless, study how he's coped with that. Is he bitter, angry, or in denial?

This father-son relationship is vital because it will likely indicate something about what kind of man he is. Some fatherless men may have emotional scars they carry around. Most people with emotional trauma don't have the physical scars to match their inner pain. I wish this were not the case. The physical scar would at minimum be a sign that the guy has been hurt and has some work to do towards healing. You have to view him honestly and recognize if his emotional wounds impede his ability to be a good mate. If he was fortunate enough to grow up with dad in the home or have a close relationship with him then you want to know what he learned about being a man, father, romantic mate, and responsible adult.

If you date or marry a man who hasn't witnessed a real man getting up and going to work to provide for his family, or doing repairs around the home or leading his family to church on Sundays, but this is what you need, then your expectations may be unreasonable. You want to see whose behavior he's learned to model and who he will bring forward in a relationship. Regardless of the type of home your man was raised in you need to see not only what he learned about being a man but most importantly if this is the kind of man you want in your life.

Fatherless boys ultimately grow up to be men. Men face great social expectations, especially from women, to become protectors and providers for their families and some men can't do this. You need to know about your partner's relationship with his father because it may give you insight on the kind of man he may be. A man who grew up without a father or a dysfunctional father/father figure may be masking some of the following issues:

- Uncertainty about social roles and responsibilities
- Self-destructive behaviors
- Anger and bitterness
- Emotionally and physically abusive towards women
- Mental instability[50]
- Emotional detachment

HE DOESN'T HAVE A FATHER

The most crucial role fathers have in the lives of their sons is to offer a model of manhood. What sons see in their fathers' social, professional, and domestic example and through their relationship with each other provides the training men need to have confidence in their

---

[50] Erickson, B. (1998). Longing for Dad: Father Loss and its Impact. Health Communications, Inc. Deerfield Beach, Florida.

abilities to be husbands and fathers. Fathers share life experiences and walk their sons through childhood into adulthood. If a young man doesn't have a dad, he too, like girls without daddies, may fill in the gaps with falsehoods and fantasies.

Research suggests that fatherless men may have some of the same symptoms as women who grow up without a dad,[51] including poor self-esteem, fear of abandonment, fear of commitment, shame, and anger. If a man has low self-esteem, he may not be comfortable with being a leader in the home. If a man feels abandoned by dad, he may struggle with giving or receiving love. If a man has absorbed his father's commitment issues, he may be afraid of commitment. If a man feels ashamed about his past, he may lie or omit crucial information about himself. If a man lacks trust, you may find yourself having to prove your whereabouts 24 hours a day. These manifestations will prevent him from being a healthy mate and the kind of man that you hopefully know you need and deserve. You definitely want to dodge the man

---

[51] Erickson, B. (1998). Longing for dad: Father Loss and its impact. Health Communications, Inc. Deerfield Beach, Florida.

whose fatherlessness is tucked away unconsciously in the back of his mind while producing some of those negative manifestations.

The story of Jessica, a young woman I met years ago, is a testament to how fatherlessness impacts men. Jessica dated Mark for several years. Mark was good-looking, physically fit, and well-educated. After dating a few months, they decided to be in an exclusive relationship but abstain from having sex. Whenever they spent the night together, Mark either slept on the floor or a futon in the same room. Jessica thought this was a gesture of the respect Mark held for their commitment. Temptation got the best of them eventually and they started having sex. When the act was over, Mark would get out of bed and lie on the floor and fall fast to sleep. This really annoyed Jessica because she wanted to cuddle and thought Mark didn't enjoy being intimate with her. He reassured her that he did.

The behavior continued over the next few weeks, and Jessica pressed Mark for an explanation. He finally broke down and explained his painful childhood. He had been abused and abandoned by his dad. Mark revealed that he hated his father whom he had not seen in decades. As a result, he had issues with trust, shame and guilt. Mark began therapy but struggled to overcome his past. Jessica even attended some sessions to understand his pain and work on their relationship. The psychologist warned Jessica that even though Mark loved her, he wasn't emotionally ready to be in a committed relationship. She initially stood by his side but after hanging on for several more months, Jessica finally realized Mark's therapist was right. Mark's problems were overwhelming, and she ended the relationship.

Countless women date or marry and assume that they will be able to depend on their boyfriends or husbands to be effective leaders or co-directors in their homes, providers, and lovers. Only their assumptions were never confirmed by their partner's behavior, character, or background. I've interviewed a lot of women over the years that are upset with their men because they are not providing them with what they expected and feel they need. The lesson to learn here is that dating gives you the opportunity to test and disprove so that you can possibly save yourself and someone else a lot of heart ache.

Chapter 7
How Will I Know If He's Worthy of Me?

How will I know if he really loves me? How will I know [don't trust your feelings]. How will I know [Love can be deceiving]. What a wonderfully catchy song! "How Will I Know" sung by the late phenomenal Whitney Houston, is a cautionary but hopeful love song from which women in the dating world can draw some lessons. Let's take a little poetic license though and consider a revision. As it is, the line, "How will I know if he really loves me?" reinforces the self-doubt and passivity that I hope this book encourages you to move away from. The line suggests a girlish woman who, not sure of her own lovability, is both insecure and longing for love and affirmation that she could be her dream guy's chosen one. It's a perfect line for a fatherless daughter who's all grown up and out there in the dating jungle, still missing the paternal love that eluded her.

What if we re-imagine that line? *How Will I Know if he's worthy of me? . . .* Written this way, the line sets you up to be discerning; your worthiness is a given, but gauging his suitability for you and his worthiness invites you to actively discern the truth. Consider those other cautionary lines, 'don't trust your feelings' and 'love can be deceiving.' Actually, you want to trust your feelings, after you've developed your ability to be discerning and done pivotal healing and work towards building a healthy self-esteem. Your instinct is a great asset, but it takes time to hone it and then respond to the signs it gives you with confidence.

> *Follow your instincts. That's where true wisdom manifests itself.* [52]—*Oprah Winfrey*

And love is not really deceiving; our feelings can be when we're too overwhelmed by emotional baggage, pain, and desperation, and people can definitely be deceiving. Though some things about a guy should be automatic red flags, a lot of you, like myself at one time, don't necessarily have a clear sense of manifestations that should make us step away from a guy or never get involved with a guy in the first place. As I've noted previously, I accepted men who treated me terribly. My desperation made me foolish as I invited untrustworthy,

---

[52] http://www.goodreads.com/quotes/115063-follow-your-instincts-that-s-where-true-wisdom-manifests-itself.

socially irresponsible men into my life because I wasn't just seeking a boyfriend and ideal husband. I was trying to fill a void that the absence of my father produced all those years ago.

UNTRUSTWORTHY

Trust is the foundation of any union. If there's no trust, there's no relationship. If you lack trust in yourself then you'll project that and likely attract the very men you don't need or really want – the untrustworthy, unreliable ones. That's exactly the situation that one woman shared with me. Jennifer's parents separated when she was in middle school. She has vivid memories of her father beating her mother. One incident repeatedly plays in her mind. Jennifer remembers her father pouring a large pot of hot water on her mother causing severe burns on her body. Jennifer's parents separated after this event. She thought her dad was a good man but had demons that influenced his behavior. Her dad promised he would continue to play an active role in her life. Jennifer rarely interacted with her dad after her parents divorced.

Jennifer started dating a guy, Jake, who had six children by five different women! He had a difficult time managing his relationship with his children and their mothers because they lived in different communities throughout the state. Jake didn't have the time or money to spend quality time with them. Jennifer would often overhear Jake lying to his children and their mothers about his work schedule so he didn't have to see them, or rather to avoid being honest about how his financial situation and car maladies and so forth made it inconvenient for him. She dismissed the lying as merely his way of avoiding the baby mamma drama that came along with seeing his children.

Jake told Jennifer he was ready for a committed relationship eight months after they began dating. She allowed him to move in with her and her young daughter. As soon as he moved in, she suspected he was cheating on her. One Saturday night, Jennifer came to my home in tears wearing her pajamas; she was visibly shaken. I had just roller set my hair and put on my night clothes. She too had rollers in her hair. She and Jake had argued. He walked out and Jennifer was overwrought at the thought that her relationship might be over. She asked me to drive her to a nightclub Jake would often go to. Now, despite my many dating hiccups, I had always taken pride in not being one of those women who resorted to literally chasing a man down and begging him to be with me except for that one aforementioned time in my early twenties when I considered it but good friends intruded. Jennifer was distraught and determined to go, and I knew she wasn't in fit condition to drive.

    I put aside my reservations. She was so upset, and I felt sorry for her. So there we were, two grown women in pajamas with rollers in our hair, roaming the streets in the middle of the night, looking for a man. We stopped by the club. I sat in the car, Jennifer went inside, but Jake wasn't there. Instead of returning to the car, Jennifer walked to a cheap hotel located beside the club and knocked on a door while I looked on, wondering what the hell she was doing. Suddenly, Jake stood in the doorway. I could hear arguing as Jake seemed to be blocking Jennifer from getting at someone in the room. I jumped out of the car and ran over to the hotel. I dragged Jennifer back to the car and drove away. I was angry with Jennifer and angrier at myself for going against my better judgment; the situation could have been dangerous for us. Jennifer had known that Jake was probably at the hotel the whole time.

On the way home, Jennifer cried. She told me that Jake had said he wanted a monogamous relationship. She kept saying that she didn't know how he could cheat and lie to her like that. She said something else too. She said Jake was acting like all the men she'd ever known – they always let her down, she said, and lied – just like her father! I tried to calm Jennifer and help her realize a few truths. I told her that she needed to focus on Jake's behavior not just his words. His behavior was more of an indicator of who he really was, and that he couldn't do to her what she didn't allow. She could always choose not to accept his cheating and lies and leave him. I also suggested that maybe it was time for her to examine why she kept getting involved with men who wounded her and if, maybe, it had something to do with some unresolved issues with her dad. She seemed truly surprised by that but interested in my suggestion. Jake and Jennifer continued living together with the same issues until she finally broke up with him for good a year later.

Jennifer's experience is unfortunately not all that uncommon. She could have spared herself time and harm had she been willing to take Jake's honest presentation of himself as an irresponsible father, liar and cheat seriously from the very beginning. It's more difficult to protect yourself sometimes when a guy is a practiced deceiver, but what's the excuse when the dishonesty is as obvious as it was in Jake's case? Why wasn't Jennifer disturbed and able to use it as a warning of what she was in for when she witnessed him repeatedly lying to his children and 'baby mamas?' On some level, she knew he was a man she couldn't expect to trust. The five different mothers of his children was evidence of that! As much as it hurt being treated the way Jake treated her, Jennifer had become indoctrinated to perceiving this behavior as normal guy behavior, beginning with her father's example.

Research suggests that men and women lie equally.[53] Sometimes people lie to fit the expected norms of their gender roles. Men lie to make themselves look better and women lie to make others feel better. Men may be untruthful to create the illusion of the perfect gentleman. They may lie to make themselves appear more credible and to protect their manhood. Therefore, men may embellish their income, educational and employment status, career choice, relationships with

---

[53] Feldman, R. (2009). The Liar in Your Life: The Way to Truthful Relationships. Harchette Book Group. New York, NY.

women, or even their sexual preference. Men may be deceitful in order to compensate for areas in which they are deficient. In a relationship, a man's lies will be more costly if you depend on him to fulfill a specific role that he's unfit to meet. For instance, if the two of you decide that he will be the primary income earner and you resign from your job to take care of home, but he has difficulty holding steady employment, or he doesn't earn as much as he said, then you have already placed yourself in a situation that's doomed to fail.

Some men believe their own hype and present it as the truth as Chelsea, a store manager in her early thirties, found out when she dated Dan. Chelsea's father walked out of her life when she was a young girl. Dan said he was a doctor. Chelsea never thought to doubt it. He seemed to possess the material possessions of someone who had done well financially. He had a beautiful home and expensive car, and he took her to some of the best restaurants in the area. She visited his home and immediately noticed all of the medical books and journals. Sometimes he would speak medical jargon and even give her medical advice about different ailments she had. He was sophisticated, smart, and attractive, the image of the father she never had but imagined. They dated six months, and Chelsea was on her way to being very much in love with Dan.

    Chelsea mentioned Dan's name to a former work acquaintance and learned that Dan wasn't a physician and he had been telling that lie for years. She confronted Dan; he insisted that he was indeed a physician. She asked for documentation, which he couldn't produce. She realized that he had been deceptive so much and for so long that he believed his own lies. Chelsea ended the relationship. She later learned Dan was named after his father who was a doctor. The car and the home she had visited belonged to his parents. Dan used his late father's accomplishments to attract women. Months later, Chelsea saw Dan at a social event and overheard him tell a group of young women he was a doctor.

    Some men may be embarrassed about the poor choices they've made or at their lack of mature choices and reveal a little bit of information at a time. I will never forget Clay, a former boyfriend. When I asked him about previous girlfriends, an ex-wife or children, he changed the subject. When we first met, he acknowledged having two children. However, over the course of three more months, he went on to reveal more children – five at least. Of course, this made me uncomfortable. I know – clear sign to get on my running shoes and never look back, but this was on my way to being wiser and before I addressed that daddy pain. I didn't entertain Clay too much longer. When I asked Clay why he wasn't honest about his children, he said he knew that he had been sexually irresponsible, and was well aware that having a lot of children was a turn off to most women.

TOO GOOD TO BE TRUE . . .

The type of deception Clay practiced is just one of the deceptions that have become all too common in the dating universe. Globalization and technological advances such as the internet and cellular telephones have forever changed how companies and people do business. As a result, an increasing number of people do business from home as independent entrepreneurs. This has created the perfect environment for men who create an illusion of who they are to attract women and even defraud them. 'Entrepreneur' can be a fancy cover for 'unemployed.' It doesn't take much to fake a business. With a computer or through a print shop, anyone can generate documents –business cards and business labels, letterhead, etc. We admire business minded-people, and especially men, that have the expertise, talent, and courage to be successful in some independent entrepreneurial way that yields financial rewards. Due to the continuing gender encoding in our sexist society, men are more readily likely to be accepted as entrepreneurs if they dress the part. Unfortunately, some know how to do this only too well. There are men out there who use the "business man" tag to manipulate women into believing they are more financially independent than they really are.

Both sexes tend to applaud the entrepreneurial spirit, understandably so. Since a common want on the man wish list for many women is a financially healthy or wealthy man, we will invest our time, emotions, and faith in men we think have this potential. We associate it with a man's ability to take care of us whether we gain financial independence or not. It's fine to date a man who has aspirations, but first you need to measure where he's been in his professional life and what that life actually looks like. There's a big difference between Mr. Potential, who is truly working on realizing his ambition and producing results through his effort, integrity, training/education and knowledge, and Mr. Pretender who is merely a wannabe entrepreneur who deceives people about his identity. Mr. Potential is in the process of "being" or moving up to the next level. He is really up and coming. Mr. Potential may not yet have arrived at the top of the game, but it's clear that he is on the verge. For instance, if Mr. Potential has career goals to become a professional actor, lawyer or physician, he should be in graduate school, undertaking training, networking and partnering with other skilled professionals in the field.

Mr. Pretender works hard at giving the appearance of someone he's not. If you date this kind of man and fall in love with him, you are investing in an illusion, the idea he has created of his identity. He may be extremely charming and very smart if he's successful in deceiving people about his professional life. Mr. Pretender is someone who may talk a lot about the future while his finances and living situation are in chaos in the present. Often, he doesn't even have the education or work experience needed to accomplish his supposed career goal or entrepreneurial vision. He talks a good game and may wear a business suit well quite literally. The following two women that I interviewed experienced relationships with men that exemplify the contrasts between a Mr. Pretender and Mr. Potential.

Janice never met her father; she didn't even know his name. She was a single mom of two small children when she met Jacob. Jacob was an attractive man in his mid-forties, who unbeknownst to Janice had an inconsistent employment history. When they met, he lived at home with his mother whom he claimed to be taking care of. Jacob dreamed of opening his own drafting business and appeared to Janice to be busy realizing that dream. He always carried a briefcase filled with paperwork. He would bring his laptop to her home to respond to client requests. He frequently excused himself to take a business call. Janet was so impressed by Jacob's 'diligence' that after six months of dating, she invested a small portion of her savings in his company. She even co-signed for a car. Over the next few months, Jacob withdrew from her. Whenever Janice asked him about their future, he reassured her that it was next on his agenda after building his business. One afternoon, Janice received several calls from the creditor demanding payment on Jacob's car. She finally, after months of dating, decided to go by his business to find out why he wasn't making payments but the building was empty.

Janice confronted Jacob about the car payments and the location of his company. He confessed that his business didn't exist at the moment. He had run out of cash to purchase the necessary inventory. Janice asked what happened to the money she gave him; he admitted to spending the money to date her. When Janice asked Jacob to return the car, he refused. She was forced to make payments until Jacob finally did agree to sell it. The car was sold for a loss, and she was responsible for the difference. Janice broke up with him.

When Sadie met Lawson, he was a recent college graduate. He was broke, but aspired to own a construction company. He worked hard all day and night pursuing clients, drafting plans and networking with others in the industry. His dream left little time for a personal relationship. He told Sadie that he wanted to be in a relationship but couldn't think about marriage until he accomplished his dream and could support his family. Lawson was honest and told Sadie that if she wanted a marriage level commitment from him at that time then he wasn't the one. Lawson told Sadie she was everything he wanted in a wife, but he understood if she needed a commitment then. Sadie saw a lot of her beloved father in Lawson. He had told her that a man should be motivated to work hard, sacrifice personally, and achieve some financial stability and success so that he was fit for a good wife.

For two years, Lawson and Sadie dated while Sadie finished a graduate degree and Lawson worked on starting his business. He attended conferences and took additional courses to perfect his knowledge of his field. Sadie helped by answering telephones, assisting with research for the business, and attending networking events with him. For five years, Lawson worked tirelessly and started a company with great potential for success. One day when Sadie was in the office filing papers, Lawson, Mr. Potential, thanked Sadie for her love and support and proposed. Of course, their age (late twenties) and status in life as young adults played a factor; Sadie may have decided differently and justifiably so had she been in her mid-thirties instead of her early twenties as she had been when she first met Lawson, and/or he had been pursuing his goal for a decade without serious progress.

Consider another real relationship that was shared with me. Briana never married; her father moved out of state, married and started a family. She rarely talks to him. Briana met Justin while working for the same company. They each had their own apartment. Brianna was very content with her job. However, Justin wanted to own an automotive shop. Due to poor credit, he wasn't eligible for a business loan so he wanted to downsize to save enough money to start his business. They had been dating for about seven months when Briana let Justin move in with her. She also told him that he didn't have to help with rent in order to save start-up costs for his business venture. However, Justin did have to contribute to the food expenses and utilities. Yet, when Justin was off work, he watched television and spent time with his friends instead of actively working on developing the business. When Briana inquired about the business, Justin became belligerent. Briana eventually stopped asking Justin about his plans and prayed that he would become motivated. It became a financial burden for Briana to take care of so many of the expenses.

Fifteen months into living together, Briana gave Justin an ultimatum, either he had to help with rent or move. Justin told her that he was in the process of writing his business plan to get a bank loan. When Briana inquired about the money saved from not paying rent and other living expenses, he confessed that there was none. He spent the money on buying electronic items and invested the rest in his car. He bought a flat screen television, car stereo, and rims – which he kept in storage. Briana was so upset she told Justin to move. She felt humiliated because she had allowed Justin to live off of her for as long as she had. If you don't know for sure that the guy you're dating really is a successful entrepreneur or business owner or fit to pursue his lofty career ambition, and that he's not a Mr. Pretender, consider some of the following warning signs:

- He has a lot of free time during business hours
- He doesn't have any clients or merchandise or products to sell
- He doesn't have business cards, letterhead, envelopes, web address and/or business email
- He borrows money from family members and friends and asks to borrow money from you
- He doesn't have business meetings (face to face or via telephone)
- He doesn't have IRS income tax returns for all the years his business has been in existence
- You never get to witness his business networking in person or interact with business partners and clients

There was a time when it was a given that a man in our culture was measured by his willingness to work and provide for his family; he was even respected for it. Though we have long lived in a society divided by class, respect was accorded to a hard-working man. In today's culture, some men don't feel any shame for not working or providing for their family; however, they still want to be respected as men. How do you respect a grown healthy man who doesn't have the inclination to work in order to be self-sufficient and help take care of his family? It is common today to need two incomes to maintain a household and family too, so the man need not to be expected to carry the full burden of meeting household financial obligations particularly when this responsibility is simply bigger than either mate can afford alone. At the time of this writing, the unemployment rate was the highest it's been in a decade, and it's even higher among black men!

When it comes to money and men I've always dated with this philosophy, I know what I earn and how I manage money but I need to see what any potential partner has to offer in terms of finances. I wanted a man who would work and contribute financially to the household. I'm not saying don't date someone who is financially challenged. There are good reasons why someone might be having reasonable, temporary financial difficulties. For instance, he may be recovering from a divorce or may have lost a job. However, if you are looking for a breadwinner or someone who can help with household expenses, a man who is financially challenged may not be for you.

    Still, there is a big difference between a man that doesn't and won't work to take care of himself and his family and one who's been stung by a financial crunch not of his own making. There are actually men that simply want to be taken care of by women, just as there are still women who want to be fully financially maintained by a man. I don't know why this is. If you have a work ethic and value handling your financial responsibilities, then you should certainly value this in any man you date. You should expect a man to have a good work ethic and take his employment seriously even if he works in a field that doesn't pay well. For some men, working a blue-collar job and doing work that doesn't get the respect of many professional careers, is beneath them, but if his choice is to not better his options through training and further education, and instead just not work and depend on you, then this should be a firm enough sign that your expectations are too low. Now, if you meet and become serious with a man when he is on his financial feet and successfully working/practicing his trade and then a lay-off or economic downshift hits him hard, then this is different. However, if a new man doesn't demonstrate that he is gainfully employed and financially responsible then you already have a signal of what to expect if you invest more of your time and future into him.

When Jean met Dave, he had fallen on hard times. Since Dave was supposedly actively seeking a job and he was a likable, well-spoken, attractive guy, she decided to go out with him. They went out several times and she picked up the tab. Yet, Dave provided Jean with other clues about his sketchy work history which she ignored. He often made comments like, "when I work" and "if I work." A working man shouldn't have this kind of attitude, let alone verbalize it so directly. Jean was so attracted to Dave and found him so funny and charming that she decided that he was a man with great potential without having any real evidence that her faith was warranted. Jean recommended that he accept an entry level position until he could find his dream job. Dave refused; such positions were beneath him. Eventually, Jean learned that since he'd dropped out of college at twenty, Dave only had about five years of actual employment in his adult life. He was thirty-one years old! He had lost cars and homes because he refused to work. She wasn't interested in a man who wouldn't want to work any job to keep his home functioning. She wanted a man with a steady employment history, and working sporadically wasn't satisfactory. The warning signs were there with Dave – he was too comfortable with her paying for dates and everything else all the time, seemed to be stuck in the same place with his job search, and there were gaps in his employment history.

I questioned Jean about why she got involved with Dave in the first place since the clues were already there, and why it took her almost a year to end it. I also asked her about her childhood family situation. Jean's father had passed when she was about five; what she remembered most vividly is that he made her laugh. When she was growing up without him, people who knew him always described him as a good man with charm and a great sense of humor. Jean's experience with Dave is another cautionary note about why we need to be more circumspect about what we like and expect in men before we become engrossed in dating.

Chapter 8
He's not *the one* if . . .

COMMITMENT LEERY

If a man is not ready to commit to a relationship move on. If a man says upfront that he doesn't want to be in a committed relationship, believe him! Don't internalize the reasons he doesn't want to commit to you. Don't hang around indefinitely waiting for him to provide you with an answer that won't change the circumstances. If he's not ready for a monogamous relationship or a serious relationship or marriage, respect his decision, accept that he knows his own mind and wants, then move on. Some women get involved with a man trying to get him to change his mind. This only causes problems in the long run. You can prepare the best home-cooked meals, give him the best sex he's ever had, buy him nice gifts, and even get pregnant. If he's not ready to be a father or husband or exclusive boyfriend, he's not going to commit to you.

Men don't commit for many reasons. There are some men who don't want to settle down because they believe there could be someone else better suited for them. There are other men who have seen people close to them break-up or divorce, and don't want to deal with the hurt and pain of a break-up. Commitment means responsibilities of paying bills and taking care of a household and children. This is a lot of work and not every man wants to do this. Sometimes, it's just that he doesn't have that level of feeling for you. It really is okay. You damage your own psyche when you stick around too long, hoping for something that he doesn't want. For women wounded by not feeling loved and valued by their fathers early on in their lives, this can be all too easy to fall into. You couldn't control the situation that led to your dad's absence and/or neglect, and you can't make your love interest into your ideal love and partner. Another beautiful woman that I interviewed, Sherri, discovered this the hard way.

Sherri met Matt through mutual friends. Matt was upfront and told Sherri he wasn't interested in a committed relationship. He just wanted to have a good time with a female companion. Matt had every quality Sherri was looking for in a man, a handsome, Christian, educated, and hardworking guy who made her laugh. Matt even got along extremely well with her family. Sherri's goal was to marry Matt. Eventually, she convinced him to move in with her and went about demonstrating to him that she would make a great wife. She took care of all his desires. She worked and contributed her share of the living expenses, cooked tasty meals, kept the house comfortable and clean, and took care of his sexual needs. To Sherri, Matt appeared to be content with their living arrangement. He never brought up the topic of marriage. However, Sherri wanted more. After a year she was more than ready for a family.

One day, Sherri planned a romantic evening. She prepared Matt's favorite meal and dressed in sexy lingerie. When he came home from work, she showered him with food, love and affection. Later in bed, Sherri told Matt that she was ready to get married and have babies. He told her that he was satisfied with their current living arrangement. He had not changed his mind. He wasn't interested in marriage or children at the present time, maybe in the future. She became upset and begged him to tell her what was wrong, and she would do whatever she could to fix it. Matt tried to assure Sherri that she was fine. She didn't believe him. Matt said he just wasn't ready for a commitment. They continued to argue over the issue for the next few months and Matt ended the relationship. Sherri blamed herself for the break-up. What Sherri really needed to do was interrogate the source of her blind determination to make Matt commit despite his honest expressions to the contrary. When we talked, Sherri shared that she had dreamed of having her own family and living a serene *Brady Bunch* family life. She too had grown up with a wonderful single mother but with no father in the picture.

SEXUALLY DANGEROUS/DECEPTIVE

Unfortunately, emotional damage isn't the only likely consequence of dating unwisely. These days, it can be literally physically dangerous – even deadly. In the last few years, there has been more open talk about men who conceal their true sexual identity and preferences. If a woman unintentionally becomes a 'cover girl'– literally used by a man to hide his hidden bisexuality or homosexuality– it is shameful and potentially emotionally devastating. However, in an era of HIV/AIDS, sexual deceit can be literally dangerous to our health – even deadly. Women must be empowered to date carefully and to take responsibility for being as discerning as possible when it comes to a date's and potential husband's true character.

J.L. King, author of "On The Down Low" states, "It's called the DL–the down low–brothers who have sex with other brothers. They're not in the closet; they're behind the closet. They are so far removed from attaching themselves and what they do to the homosexual lifestyle that these men do not consider themselves gay."[54] Regardless of whether or not some men are in denial about their sexuality because of fear of being ostracized socially or by family and close friends, you don't deserve to be a victim of this kind of deceit. Sometimes, because of those issues I've discussed, we can be complicit in a man's deceit because our desire for love and a happy ending blinds us to the flashing signals we receive along the way. I'm sharing the most painful romantic relationship that I ever experienced here as a perfect example and a warning to you.

I discovered the down-low phenomenon firsthand. The man on the down-low identifies himself as straight, but has sex with men on the side without disclosing this to his female sexual partners or girlfriend or wife. I had always functioned under the assumption that if a man

---

[54] J. L. King (2004). On The Down Low: A Journey Into the Lives of 'Straight' Black Men Who Sleep with Men. Harlem Moon. Broadway Books. United States.

asked me out he was heterosexual. I never considered anything else. I was terribly wrong. John and I met in our first year of graduate school. He was handsome, charming, ambitious and driven. We had similar backgrounds. We were raised in single-parent households in low-income communities. We were both determined to change our economic situation and firmly believed that education was our gateway to financial freedom. When we met it was instant chemistry. In short order, John's voice became the first one I heard every morning on the telephone and the last I heard every night. We spent a lot of time together going to the movies and out to dinner. We supported each other academically, discussing research projects and papers. We became inseparable.

When we first started dating, John had shared his perspective about sex and dating. He wanted to practice his religious beliefs and wait until he found the right woman and be engaged before he had sex. I respected his decision and accepted his explanation. I too wanted to wait until I found the right man and be in a committed relationship before I had sex. I felt blessed to have such a strong, unique, true Christian guy. Although I lived alone, at first John never spent the night at my place. He always went home. He had a roommate, Manny, who was also a graduate student. I spent time at John's home, but he always made sure that I would leave his place prior to Manny's arrival. He said they had a rule: keep guests to a minimum and no sleepovers. I respected their agreement.

One evening, John and I were sitting on the sofa working on a class assignment and the roommate walked in. Manny walked past us and didn't say a word. John asked me to leave, and I began gathering my books and papers in silence. Manny never acknowledged my presence. Manny wasn't how I had imagined him either. To be honest, he fit the stereotype of a homosexual, like Jack on that not so old television show, *Will & Grace.* And he was a dead ringer for the gay choir director that everyone whispered about [outside of church] when I was a teen, long, pressed straight hair, arched eyebrows, and super-tight bright pants. I felt uncomfortable and guilty for having these thoughts; I didn't want to judge someone I hadn't even met.

On the short drive home, I wondered why I had to leave, and why Manny had ignored me and why John allowed it. We were an adult couple, and it was still early in the evening so it wasn't like I was interrupting dinner or spending the night. The next morning I questioned John about his roommate. John said he met Manny through the university's housing program for graduate students and that he didn't know that much about him except where he was from and his graduate program of study. I didn't probe any further. I should have. It didn't make sense, and I felt uneasy about it, but I loved John and loved us. He was the kind of guy I had always wanted to marry.

However, the Manny encounter didn't exist in a vacuum. Right around the same period in our relationship, I had begun to notice that John felt uncomfortable spending intimate time together. I was accepting of this at first, and I was supportive of not having a sexual relationship. I figured that he was trying to avoid getting into a tempting situation. Still, I craved some intimacy – kissing, hugging and falling asleep in each other's arms. Whenever we embraced, John would pull away citing his vow to remain celibate. It went on this way for six more months, and I grew more frustrated. One evening, John and I went out to dinner and a movie. It was around 10 p.m. when we arrived back to my place and I invited him in. We cuddled and fell asleep in my bed. Around midnight, he jumped up in a hurry to get home. I argued with him. We were single and grown; there was no reason for him to rush home, but he left anyway. I was tired, confused, and more frustrated.

John called early the next morning as if nothing had happened. I brought up his abrupt departure, but he claimed he liked to sleep in his own bed. I felt uneasy about his explanation and finally started withdrawing a bit from the relationship, but for the wrong reason. I really started to believe something was wrong with me. There was something about me that John wasn't attracted to, but he wouldn't tell me. My time with John coincided with a time when there began to be growing rumors circulating about the disproportionate number of men on campus who were bisexual. I started thinking about John's roommate and how John had rushed away from me in the middle of the night as if he were trying to make it home by curfew. I was furious. I confronted John. I told him about the rumors, and then I just came out and asked.

"Are you gay?"

He said, "Well, I understand how you reached this conclusion about me."

"What kind of answer is that, John?"

"I understand how you reached the conclusions about me that you did," he repeated.

I hung up the telephone. That was the last time I talked to John. A few weeks later, I found out from Joel, a popular guy on campus who was also gay, that John and Manny had been lovers for years. I was livid. It took years for me to recover from this experience. It changed the way I dated. I placed almost every man I encountered on what I called the "suspect list." I know this wasn't fair, but the men I dated had to prove to me they were straight. I must admit this wasn't popular and turned men off because of the abrupt, intimidating, and hostile way that I went about it. It was great that I became more circumspect, but I also became paranoid rather than merely questioning and listening to my instincts. A close friend recommends that all women incorporate the 3-date rule when determining whether a man desires an intimate relationship with you: if he doesn't try to lure you into having sex by the 3rd date, he's not sexually interested. Red flag for the naïve. At this point, I still had not come to the realization that I needed to confront how the distance in my relationship with my father had impacted my interaction with men and the difficulty that I was having exercising consistent common sense, discernment, and faith rather than doubting myself and becoming distrustful.

My experience may have been different from other women who dated men on the down-low. Homosexuality is still a controversial issue within our culture. John, a professional, closeted homosexual black male didn't want to risk being ostracized in his personal, social, and professional life. I filled a role for him by providing him with credibility as a heterosexual man. I was John's cover girl! I should have listened to the signs earlier. Sometimes the signs aren't as overt. Some men do have sex, even good sex, with the girlfriend, wife, or sexual partner who is unknowingly a cover girl. It's a good idea for women to actually spend more time educating themselves before they jump full force into the dating jungle. Bonnie Kaye's book, "Straight Talk: A Checklist For Women Who Wonder," is a good start. She offers a list of warning signs that your guy might be lying about his sexual identity, including the following:

- You have a normal sexual appetite, but your mate thinks you have excessive sexual needs.
- There is a decline of sexual activity early in your relationship.
- Your partner is repulsed by normal sexual activity.

- Your mate admits to having had more than two homosexual encounters.
- Your partner reveals he's bisexual.
- Your mate makes continual homophobic comments.

ADDICTED TO DRUGS, SEX, ETC.

Addictions are not only harmful to your partner but impact the lives of people around him. Oftentimes, we women get early tell-tale signs that the nice cute guy we are attracted to might have an addiction.[55] People who have alcoholism or abuse alcohol often:

- Continue to drink, even when health, work, or family are being harmed
- Drink alone
- Become violent when drinking
- Become hostile when asked about drinking
- Are not able to control drinking–unable to stop or reduce alcohol intake
- Make excuses to drink
- Miss work or school, or have a decrease in performance because of drinking
- Stop taking part in activities because of alcohol
- Need to use alcohol on most days to get through the day
- Neglect to eat or eat poorly
- Do not care about, or ignore, how they dress or whether they are clean
- Try to hide alcohol use

---

[55] http://www.ncbi.nlm.nih.gov/pubmedhealth/PMH0001940/.

- Shake in the morning or after periods when they have not had a drink

You ignore the fact that even the night you met, he was partying hard and drinking a lot and the next time you saw him it was the same thing, or you ignore that he always seems to be down for getting a drink or requires that as a part of any social evening. Or he actually smoked a joint around you though he said he only did it occasionally. One of the biggest problems with addictions is that the person with the problem is often in denial. Part of your early conversation with a new man should revolve around discussing each other's history, attitudes, and current alcohol and drug use. People certainly conceal the truth about drug use and their drinking habits and sexual history; that's why we need to be good detail recorders and observers. If you are a woman whose family and parental relationship was impacted by say the alcoholism of dad, then you need to examine this impact on your life and be aware of signs of these problems in the men you date. Let's look at Cassandra and Anthony. Cassandra's father died of a drug overdose when she was a little girl. She has vague memories of him.

Cassandra met Anthony at a nightclub. Their relationship formed quickly. They were a very social couple and partied almost every weekend. Whenever they went out, they always consumed alcohol. They would drink and party until the wee hours of the morning, get a few hours' sleep and then go to work. Cassandra didn't see this as a problem because they were functional. Sometimes, Anthony would smoke marijuana. She didn't like it, but it was only occasionally and it was not a big part of his life. Anthony also hung out frequently with his drinking buddies.

They dated for about two years and then got married. Cassandra assumed that when they married, Anthony would eliminate some of his social outings, drinking and sporadic use of drugs. She was wrong. He continued to drink and smoke marijuana after the birth of their son two years later. Anthony's drinking and drug use escalated. He began using crack cocaine. He used household funds to finance his habits. He started missing work and spending more time in bars. He was negligent in paying bills, and utilities were being disconnected. It was typical for Cassandra to come home from work to find Anthony passed out with a bottle in his hand.

His behavior, appearance, and once light-hearted demeanor changed. Whenever Cassandra confronted Anthony about the drinking and drugs, he became angry. On one occasion, Anthony hit Cassandra in the face in front of their son. She threatened to leave him if he didn't get help. She spoke to his mom and encouraged her to get him to re-enter another rehab facility; he did. Anthony came home and everything was fine for a while. He was sober, got a job, and spent time with his family. However, within six months, he started hanging out with his old friends and engaging in the same problematic behavior. Meanwhile, Cassandra found herself financially strapped and emotionally drained. She went through this cycle with Anthony for several years until she reached the conclusion that she didn't want her son to accept his father's behavior as normal, and she was tired of the financial strain and the physical and emotional abuse. Cassandra filed for divorce. She finally realized that she couldn't save Anthony from himself. Imagine the grief she could have avoided, had she paid attention to the early signs.

SOMEBODY ELSE'S HUSBAND

If that new great guy in your life doesn't take you to public places, or if he does but takes you to what he calls his "special place," then he might be married. If he doesn't invite you around his family members and close friends though you take him around your intimate circle, he only wants to spend time at your place, never invites you to his home, or is only available at peculiar times or in very limited time and you know for sure it's not due to his government job then face it, he just may be somebody else's guy already. There are some married men who actively date and conceal their married status. Beware! If you meet a married man who is looking for an extramarital affair or unknowingly date a man and later find out he's married, RUN!

Linda's parents never married. She didn't have a relationship with her father at all. Whenever Linda reached out to him, he rejected her so she just gave up. Linda met Mack at a networking event for professionals. They exchanged business cards and agreed to meet for dinner within the next week. Mack pursued Linda. He called her every day until she confirmed a date. Mack said he was single with a young daughter who lived with her mother in his hometown which was about two hours away. Mack said he visited his hometown most weekends to spend time with his daughter and help his parents who owned a catering business. Since Linda had just moved to the area and was keeping her initial dating options open, they would meet for lunch and sometimes go out to dinner. Mack always took her to the same restaurant. She thought it was a little odd but assumed he was just a creature of habit. He always paid, so she never complained and they always had a nice time. Linda and Mack even ran into each other while they were on dates with other people. However, as they spent more time together, Linda eventually invited him to her home. Mack gave Linda the name of his neighborhood, but never invited her to his home. Whenever Linda asked about visiting his home, he dismissed it by saying, his home was a bachelors' pad and untidy. At the time, Linda didn't think to question his explanation and took him at his word.

  Linda and Mack agreed to have a monogamous relationship and became sexually intimate. One night, after a sexual encounter, they fell asleep in each other's arms. Mack woke up about 3:00 a.m. in a panic. He jumped up and got dressed in a hurry. Linda asked him what was wrong and he said he had to get home. She was confused. Days passed and she didn't hear from Mack. Linda wondered if maybe she hadn't satisfied him sexually. He finally called. He said that he had just been hired at a new firm and was studying for an exam for his new position. He sounded a little distant as if he didn't want to talk and he didn't provide an explanation for rushing out of her home.

    To show her support for his new job, Linda decided to send him a basket of goodies to eat while preparing for his test. She looked him up in the white pages and saw Mrs. listed by his name. She was upset. She called the number listed, and Mack answered the telephone. He was shocked. Linda asked Mack if he had a wife and he said that he was unhappily married. He had the nerve to ask if they could continue seeing each other because he liked hanging out together. She was the distraction he needed from his marital problems. Mack told Linda he was going out of town on business and he wanted her to join him so he could explain his home life. She was appalled and told him to never contact her again. Linda was hurt because she had unknowingly had an intimate relationship with a married man. To make matters worse, he was spending his household funds on pursuing her.

Linda was aware of the weekend he was going out of town so she took it upon herself to call his wife. If it were her, she'd want to know her husband was a serial dater/cheater. Linda dialed the telephone and his wife answered. She could hear an infant who was cooing in the background. Her heart sank, not only was Mack cheating but he had a newborn child. Even though she never met his wife, she felt sorry for her. Linda identified herself and apologized. Mack's wife said that Linda wasn't the first. The wife asked for specific dates and times and Linda provided the information. The wife asked if they had protected sex and Linda said yes. The wife thanked Linda for calling.

When Mack returned from his business he contacted Linda and wanted to know why she called his wife. Linda told Mack that she was looking for a husband and since he was already married he didn't meet her eligibility requirements. Mack asked if they could still be friends. Linda hung up the telephone. That was the last time she talked to Mack. A few months later she saw him at a nightclub socializing with women. As a woman out there dating with the goal or hope of getting married, you know how rough it is out there. Think of yourself as a wife; would you want to be a wife whose husband goes out dating as if he is a single man? If you grew up in a home where this was a problem or you witnessed a parent cheating or your own dad cheated on your mom, you carry some pain about this. Remember that this pain makes you vulnerable and you might wind up being hurt by the same kind of behavior.

RELIGIOUSLY/SPIRITUALLY CONTENTIOUS

I tried to lead a man to Jesus and failed miserably. If you believe in God and you date a partner who is a non-believer, or if he challenges and doubts God's existence but promises that he's open to receiving God or attending church regularly, your relationship may very well be doomed from the very beginning. Don't dismiss this important difference between you and think you can change him. If a man says, "I'm not opposed to going to church," or "I didn't say I don't believe in God, I just don't go to church," you become hopeful, thinking that you can convert him into a believer. That's exactly what I tried to do. I mentioned Joseph earlier. He was very angry, bitter and mean. He rarely had anything nice to say. His disposition, his words, his heart and attitude were negative. Joseph had a sharp tongue and would spew out words that felt like flames. He taught me a lot of valuable life lessons. I was so taken with our physical chemistry, and impressed with his academic accomplishments (a doctorate in economics), high-earning career (corporate finance), sophistication, and some of our shared non-religious views that I deceived myself into believing that this compensated for our differing spiritual and religious orientation. And I thought he'd come around since sometimes Joseph's belief in God tended to waver. One day he was a believer and the next day he questioned God's existence. He was trying to determine whether or not God had a place in his life. This should have been a clue for me to move on but I didn't. Since Joseph just didn't come out and reject God, I thought I could convert him into a believer in Jesus Christ. I was dead wrong!

Joseph knew the Bible inside and out and would often take scriptures out of context. He used the Bible to badger others who loved the Lord. I hated this! We completely differed in fundamental beliefs about our existence as human beings as we did about God's role in it. I was a faithful church-going member. I grew to dread the weekends because I knew we would argue over me going to church Sunday morning. Once I asked him to join me for church on Easter Sunday. He explained to me that with my level of education, I should know that Jesus couldn't be real. We had a heated debate. At that moment, I realized that he believed what he believed and I couldn't change his mind. I walked towards the door to leave his apartment and heard an object hit the door. He had thrown the control panel of an electric blanket at me and missed. When I turned around, he said, "I don't want a woman who chooses God over me. If you leave don't come back." I opened the door and walked out with a sigh of relief. It was over. By this time, Joseph had worn me out mentally and physically. Trying to convert someone is a lot of hard work. He continued to call me, but I really didn't have anything to say to him, and we never went out again. To this day, I'm so grateful that I had the courage to walk away. I dated him too long when it was clear that our differing core beliefs should've been a date breaker from the beginning!

It is definitely better to select a man who shares the same religious or spiritual orientation that you have. Some couples come together and build effective relationships despite their differing religious backgrounds. This requires that each of you have a deep knowledge of and respect for each other's spiritual and/or religious beliefs and the ability to compromise about how your family life will accommodate these if you both practice the religious principles and rituals of your faith. Be honest about how important this is to you in a mate. If you passionately believe in God then ideally you want your partner to already have an established relationship with God as well. It's naive to think you can lead your partner to love the Lord the same way that you do. You also don't want a partner who is going through the motions and attending church to win you over. You want to see your partner's faith during adversity. You want a partner who sees God as an integral part of your relationship. Settling for someone who is not evenly yoked only creates chaos and confusion.

> *When you choose a mate be absolutely sure to obey the instructions God gives in 2 Corinthians 6:14-15: 'Be ye not unequally yoked together with unbelievers: for what fellowship hath righteousness with unrighteousness? and what communion hath light with darkness? And what concord hath Christ with Belial? or what part hath he that believeth with an infidel?' In other words, only marry a believer. Unpopular though it sometimes may be among singles, that is a requirement of God. Keep it without compromise. If you're dating a man who is 'kind of saved,' who drinks a little and smokes a little and cusses a little, then get*

> *rid of him until he gets delivered from that little bit of stuff he's been doing. You don't need to marry into that mess. You wait until he gets 'real saved' before you marry him. Even then don't rush into anything. Take time to observe that potential mate very carefully. They are not always what they appear to be. Just because they say they're a Christian, don't automatically believe it.* [56] —Creflo Dollar

A religious or spiritual man will exhibit deeds based on his beliefs. Spending time with your partner in his church home is a must. One particular research study identifies 13 common life principles people learn by religious or spiritual foundation, regardless of denomination. These principles are common in most religions.[57] The principles are: meditation; prayer; belief that life has purpose; accepting themselves and others for who they are; living ethically; living life knowing you are part of something larger and greater than self; knowing how to forgive; volunteering and acts of charity; having religious and spiritual paradigms, which give worshipers exemplars to imitate when in a challenging situation such as asking, "What would Jesus do?;"

---

[56] Creflo, D. Til Death Do You Part Is a Long, Long Time: http://ww.kcm.org/index.php?p=real_help_content&id=1095.
[57] Plante, T. (2008). What Might Spirituality and Religion Offer the Contemporary Practicing Psychologist? http://www.psychologytoday.com/files/attachments/34033/pp2article.pdf.

reading the Bible and other self-improvement books; having self-esteem; having community support; being able to think outside of yourself, for example, thinking of ways to improve the lives of the poor. Therefore, having a partner who is of the same denomination may not be as important as having someone who is a believer.

A COSTLY DATE

Dating can be an exciting but expensive endeavor. It is not uncommon for most couples to share dating costs. Typical dating expenses may include dinner, movies and maybe some type of physical activity such as dancing, bowling, or roller skating. As the relationship progresses you may do some traveling or celebrate the holidays together. These expenses are fine as long as your partner is pulling his weight. Keep this in mind if you're actively seeking a husband who is also a provider. If a man is struggling financially to take you to the movies and out to dinner, he can't take care of an entire household.

Some fatherless daughters pay their partner's rent, car and child support payments, his utilities and charge his personal items and living expenses on their credit cards. These are not dating expenses but marital household obligations. If you find yourself placing your partner in your budget, you may want to re-evaluate your relationship.

I had a general rule of spending about $1,200 per calendar year on casual dating, which averaged $100 per month. I refer to this as getting acquainted dates such as dinner, movies, picnics or general entertainment. This did not include trips or weekend getaways. This is the amount I felt comfortable with for my income level and was reasonable for me. Sometimes I exceeded my budget but an established dollar amount gave me parameters to work within.

If your expenses are more than you allocated in your budget you need to ask yourself if you have a partner or a liability. Never put yourself in a situation in which you are paying his major bills. Also, be cautious of men who want you to invest your money first and he promises that he will pay your money back, or men who want you to cosign or sign for loans.

I met Thomas in a department store. He was well dressed in expensive clothes. He invited me to his home and his place looked like it had been designed by an interior decorator. However, he had done the work himself. I could tell he invested a lot of time and money in his home. So I assumed his finances were together. I had been dating Thomas for less than three months and he was quite ambitious. His goal was to open a retail store. He had all of the elements needed to implement his plan. He identified a location, employees and had access to merchandise. He even introduced me to a couple who owned a similar store and they were also his mentors. I was quite impressed. He was missing one key component. He had bad credit and needed a co-signer. I guess this is where I came in. He had defaulted on his student loans, had a car repossessed, unpaid rent and a host of other outstanding debt.

Thomas asked me to take out a $50, 000 loan and he would pay me back once he generated profit from his store. Remember, I had a dating budget of $1,200 per year so his request exceeded my available funds by $48,800. I immediately told him no. He did everything he could to persuade me to say yes. This was a lot to ask since we had just started dating. He even asked me to marry him. Although I was thrilled at the proposal, I insisted that we continue dating and revisit the topic of marriage in a year. He agreed.

But more importantly, I wanted to know more about his financial history and if he was working to repair it. My belief is when a man asks for money he should be willing to disclose his financial information. And, this provides an opportunity to discuss his financial philosophy, long-term financial goals, retirement plans, and whether we were financially compatible. So I asked him for his financial history income, paystubs, credit reports, current debt level, etc. Thomas was upset with me for asking about his finances. We went back and forth for weeks about this. He presented some of the documents I requested and gave me the rest at a later time. When I reviewed his paperwork I had more questions than answers and he was reluctant to discuss my concerns in great detail. He eventually stopped asking me for money and about a year later we broke up. Here are some signs that your partner may be experiencing financial problems:

- He brags about money but doesn't have anything to show for it
- He doesn't have a checking or savings account
- He bounces checks
- He asks for a loan and promises to repay within a few days
- He doesn't pay for dates
- He borrows money from family, friends, coworkers
- He lives beyond his means
- He receives telephone calls from creditors
- He's anxious to be married

- He only discusses his finances in general terms and does not give specific details
- He promises to pay you back as soon as his business makes money

Chapter 9
DATING PREP 101

You hopefully now have a clearer understanding of the poor dating choices that fatherless women make and a better understanding of the kinds of men you want to eliminate from your dating and potential mate pool. Now I want to give you some specific pointers on what you need to explore during the dating process. These can help you better determine if a man is fit for a deeper dating and relationship commitment. As I mentioned earlier, one of my biggest mistakes is that I focused on a man's personality (he made me laugh, his interest in reading, or traveling) and physical attributes (his six pack, great hair, beautiful eyes) when I should have focused on his character and discovering more about his emotional health, intrinsic qualities, and long-term relationship goals.

Character, yours and his, is the foundation that allows your relationship to grow and flourish. Character is the moral or ethical compass that guides our lives. A man's character determines how he not only values himself and behaves, but how he will treat you, children, and your family and friends. Character counts! A man's character is basically the blueprint of your relationship and determines whether or not your union will be weak or strong, filled with joy or with sorrow. In order to learn the nature of a man's character, you must learn his value system.

I would be a wealthy woman if I had a dollar every time I've heard women say, "He acts like a child" or "I feel more like his mother than his girlfriend." I've interviewed women who had immature boyfriends and husbands. Their lives were always the same, that is, filled with frustration and anger. They had chosen selfish men. One of these women, Leslie, related her relationship story. One time Aiden took their rent money to buy rims for his car. Another time, Aiden splurged and treated himself to a big screen television with the money they had been saving to buy their child a bed. He placed his individual wants and desires above his family. He even spent grocery money on playing golf with his friends.

I wouldn't recommend committing to a relationship until you've thoroughly investigated his thinking and ability to think critically about not only his philosophy of life but attitudes about individual and family responsibility. His maturity and ability to reason in regards to these things are critical to establishing an effective relationship. His behavior should emulate his thinking. Both his stated thinking and behavior communicate the level of his maturity. Women who are looking for someone to be a leader in the home should examine the evidence of this in a man while dating. A mature man has the basic tools to fill his responsibilities and the potential to evolve even more. An immature man requires basic help and doesn't own or necessarily see basic responsibilities as his to assume. You should be concerned to know whether the guy is a rational or irrational thinker. How does he formulate ideas or reach conclusions? Examining his maturity level from this perspective will allow you to see how he reasons, plans, solves problems, comprehends and learns new information. The mature man takes others into consideration in decision making. He is thoughtful with his time, money and resources, but an immature man has a tendency to be self-centered. His ultimate aim may likely be to maximize what he can get, and he doesn't think about how his actions impact others at all.

Relationships with family, friends and community are important to the emotionally mature man. The mature man values people and works hard at maintaining relationships; if by chance, a disagreement occurs this person knows how to forgive. The immature man has a difficult time being loyal and trusting anyone. If a relationship is not going well, the immature man places all of the blame on the other person. The immature man is not committed to working through problems and may be prone to walk. He may have very chaotic relationships and a history of broken friendships and relationships because of perceived slights and betrayals.

Don't assume that every man over 18 years of age possesses the emotional maturity to fulfill all of the responsibilities of marriage. Some people age chronologically but don't mature emotionally. It's imperative that you can discern the differences between the two. Why? Emotionally immature people may have a great surface appearance and be articulate, professionally successful, and gifted in areas and still be too emotionally immature to be in a committed relationship with you. You may not have had a father or positive paternal – like figure who modeled what emotional maturity in a man might look like, but if you know what to look out for, you can be empowered to choose your relationships wisely.

When it comes to love, mature men are secure rather than possessive, able to give and receive, and perceive love as a reciprocal relationship. The immature man demands love and affection. He may guilt you into feeling sorry for him by saying "You are the only person in my life," "No one loves me," or "Don't reject me like my parents." He may even tell you a sad event such as an untimely death of a parent or spouse, being abused as a child, or being in a drug-infested environment so that you will feel sad and desirous of doing anything to make him feel love. If you've been longing for love due to the absence of a dad in your life or you had a dad who was emotionally immature in some or all these ways, you really need to be aware of how this might have affected your vulnerability to such a man.[58]

HOW HE MANAGES HIS EMOTIONS

Mature men are able to control and direct their emotions into proper channels. If he is frustrated, he may exert energy by competing in a game of basketball to work off tension, or he may exercise for relief.

---

[58] http://www.sonic.net/~drmurray/maturity.htm.

Once emotions are calm he may promptly start working on a solution to the problem. An immature man can't handle frustration and experiences mood swings and temper tantrums. He lashes out if he doesn't get his way. If he is hurt, the immature man holds on to negative emotions and even if he receives an apology he holds onto grudges and doesn't forgive. In contrast, some of the traits that suggest emotional maturity in a man include his ability to accept constructive criticism, problem solving, direct his negative emotions into constructive and harmless outlets, and forgive. You should pay close attention and be concerned if the guy you begin dating can't handle criticism, has mood swings, and displays jealousy of others and irrational fear and/or anger.

HOW HE MANAGES FINANCES

Not to belabor a point well-addressed by now, but mature men fulfill their financial responsibilities. Select someone who is conscientious about his credit. If he has poor personal finance management skills then don't expect him to develop them because you date him or if you get married. If he's being chased by creditors, ignores bills, and struggles to pay for the basic necessities of life like electric, water, gas, etc., and that is his normal pattern, then you already have a warning signal that he's not the one. A socially and emotionally mature man can handle delayed gratification. He can set long-range goals and work towards accomplishing them. If he has a mature, grown-up understanding of adult responsibility then he grasps the value of saving long-term for retirement and the purchase of a home. The opposite kind of guy doesn't believe in delayed gratification, and he will probably have difficulty setting goals and working wisely to accomplish them.

The causes of emotional immaturity are varied. A number of theories suggest that it may develop from some type of trauma like death, divorce, parental abandonment, death of a loved one, pre-birth issues such as maternal addictions, too strict or poor parenting, abuse, and neglect. Not everyone exposed to these negative behaviors and/or environments become immature adults, of course, but some people don't heal from their pain.

This is why consciously studying a man's emotional maturity before you form a serious emotional attachment and invest possibly years of your time is so important. Unfortunately, love is not enough if you fall in love with an immature man. You can't make him grow up or complete him. This sort of guy will generally be high maintenance and require assistance from a host of community resources such as counselors, therapists and job agencies. It is also difficult for an immature man to realize that he needs help. I dated Marcus when I was a senior in high school, and he was about 21 years old. Marcus was a light-skinned black man with "good hair." I thought we could make beautiful babies. Remember I was naïve in my relationship choices, though I always understood the importance of going to college and achieving on my own. We both grew up in economically disadvantaged communities and realized that a formal education was our best route to financial freedom.

I worked part-time at a fast food restaurant to save money for college expenses. Marcus worked full-time to save for college while he lived with his mother. I assumed we really were on the same track, but it turned out that what he had was the idea of going to college rather than the maturity to plan for it wisely. Whenever he got paid, he spent money on clothes, and he even went out and bought a car that was too expensive for a college-bound student. He created expenses that would be difficult to maintain as a full-time college student. There were even a few times he would ask me for money to support his spending habits. I reminded him that I was working to go to college and that he needed to save his money for school as well. I never gave him any money and he became frustrated. We argued over what he needed to do with his paycheck. I found myself in the role of the parent and not that of a supportive girlfriend. When it came time to pay fees and deposits for school, he didn't have any money. Marcus even got to the point where he would spend his money on partying and alcohol and neglect to pay his own bills. The one thing that I did appreciate about my too distant father growing up was that I knew he did value wise money management and saving, and handling his financial responsibilities, including child support.

  I didn't have time to continuously tell Marcus to save his money so he could better himself. I realized that I wanted him to have a better life more than he did. This was a daily struggle and became overwhelming after a while. I needed to keep the focus on my dreams of a college education. About a week before I went away to school, we decided to end our relationship. I saw Marcus about a decade later and he looked like life had not been kind to him. He had aged poorly. He still talked about going to college and moving out of his mother's house. He had difficulty finding steady employment and he had the same financial problems. And to make matters worse, he now had children by different moms and couldn't make his child support obligations. Although he was in his early thirties then he was not making mature choices. Can you imagine our struggles if we had married? If a man is immature there's absolutely nothing you can do about it, but pray for him.

Chapter 10
Dating: A Fact Finding Expedition

The goal in dating is to identify a man who has the positive qualities you desire to build a healthy loving relationship. There is little reason to think that if you get married you won't see the same problematic behaviors evidenced while dating. This is why you need to have clarity about what you need as well as desire in a man before you enter into a relationship. Take your time during the dating phase to see if he meets your needs. The dating phase is when you should investigate key aspects of his life, especially those areas which are most important to you. For example, if you want a working man who can financially contribute to the household then check this quality out closely while you're interacting with him and dating. If it's important to you to have a mate who can and does clean up after himself in the home, then you should visit his home periodically and observe and discuss his attitudes about this and shared housework. Again, if your boyfriend or steady date doesn't possess what you need during the dating period, these qualities will not just pop up in marriage. Relationships don't work like that.

A close friend of mine had been married only a few weeks but suspected that her husband was having an affair with an ex-girlfriend. She was familiar with his behavior of cheating because he did this while they were dating. He would start arguments over petty issues so he could justify staying out all night. When she confronted him about his behavior, he would retort, "You knew what kind of man I was when we dated. You can't expect me to stop now that we're married." He's right. This is why you should have more than vague notions and surface ideas about your standards for men you date. Dr. Phil McGraw is famous for saying, "The best predictor of future behavior is relevant past behavior." This simply means, if a man exhibits a pattern of cheating on you during the dating phase he may cheat on you during your marriage.

Dating is more than social outings (going out to dinner or the movies, etc.), talking on the phone all night, flirting through texts, and hanging out, cuddling and having sex and feeling sort of high on the mix of sexual chemistry and the excitement of having someone attractive in your life. If this is pretty much your perspective of romantic relationships, you're not set up to get to know a man as thoroughly as you should before you invest yourself in a relationship with him. I know the idea might be novel and even a bit intimidating or scary, but as a grown woman, fatherless or not, you have the power to invite or un-invite a man into your life and personal space. You can exercise wisdom and thus significantly safeguard your time and well-being. To do this, you must look at dating as a process for healthy assessment and evaluation, accomplished through collecting information, analyzing it, then formulating reasonable conclusions that you can and do act upon. This kind of approach will help you improve your instincts if they're shaky and develop your ability to trust in your instincts.

Remember that often in dating both men and women give their best presentation of self. This is often accomplished through adopting expected, stereotypical gender behaviors; this isn't bad. It's just that it can be a performance masking the fact that underneath the surface the person may seriously lack the character traits that you value, and those that may be expected generally with socially as well as emotionally mature individuals. In this and the next couple of chapters, I want you to open your mind to what might be a new way of thinking about dating and your role in dating. *Dating is a fact-finding expedition*. This is useful for all women to understand and for women who may have issues with fear, loneliness, and self-esteem overcoming the absence, abuse, or neglect of their fathers. It is critical. Some men are open and honest and share their plans and some men may keep their true self and motives hidden.

During the dating process, you're supposed to uncover useful details and clues about your partner. Dating is the time to get more than a cursory glance of his true character and identity. Is he honest? Does he have a work ethic? Is he independent? Does he have any bad habits such as addictions and illegal activities? Who are his friends? What kind of friends does he have? What is his employment history? How are his finances? Is he a man of integrity? Is he heterosexual? Is he bi-sexual? What is his relationship like with his mother? What are his goals and dreams? Does he have any children? How does he treat them? What type of relationship does he have with the child's mother? Has he been married? If he's been married, why did they divorce? Does he want to be married? Can he be monogamous? I know it's a lengthy list of questions and there are more.

Once I became wiser in my dating, I learned how to obtain useful information. For example, not too long before I started dating my husband, I went out with this guy William several times. By that time, I felt comfortable enough with him to share my dating standards. I mentioned that I wanted a husband who came home at night. William laughed and said he wasn't the kind of man who could promise coming home to a wife every night. I was glad William was honest with me and more pleased that I had become wise enough to make that our last date.

REASONABLE DATING REQUIREMENTS

I mentioned before that I used to have some superficial dating standards along with some that were more valuable. I've interacted with a lot of women and listened to all too familiar conversations about their expectations or standards for men they want to date and/or marry. Oftentimes, the first discussed revolves around desired income and educational level. Now, let me make clear that this is not to suggest that the women were motivated by wanting to be financially taken care of by a man. Frequently, these conversations occurred among financially independent, professionally successful and well-educated women. The women wanted an equal partner. They also desired to protect themselves from predators that were out there looking for women to take care of them, and many, unfortunately, had dealt too often with men who were threatened by their education and success, so they did not want to deal with that.

It was not surprising then, that this attribute was foremost in their minds. However, hardly any conversations about standards involved more precise key elements about a potential mate's temperament, emotional health, family background, ethics, and so forth. And the latter should be covered more specifically than just by adding 'Christian' and church-going' to the list. You can't ask the right questions and deeper questions, if you don't get specific about the qualities that are important to you. For instance, if you have traditional values and believe in sex only in marriage, or you don't want to date someone who expects you to pay for dates, don't wait until the 5th date or so without having shared your views and asked about his. Don't get offended if he asks you to share the dating costs or for sex. This needs to be discussed early rather than later. It allows you and him as well to make thoughtful decisions about continuing to date or not. As a woman who didn't get to benefit from some of the confidence and security that

I believe a more positive daughter-father relationship would have encouraged, I lacked the confidence and sense of empowerment to articulate some of my important views and expectations and lacked even more the courage to inquire about the man's. I was too afraid that the guy I was attracted to and interested in would disappear or reject me.

This could be true of you too. Part of my aim with this book is to help you to formulate questions to ask men during the dating phase and empower you to ask them and respond proactively to the answers. Think of these as "qualifier" questions that should be asked within the first several dates. Qualifier questions will help you determine if he possesses what you're looking for in a partner so you don't waste time and endanger your future. Most of these queries do not invoke "yes" or "no" responses. They require some in-depth explanation. The responses should provide you insight about who he is and tell you about his communication style as you absorb both his verbal and nonverbal cues.

His responses, particularly those that fit your expectations, should be verifiable through his behavior. In other words, his words and behavior should match. Beyond standard dating questions, about age, job or profession, marital, and relationship status and do you have children, be sure to broach such questions as what is your perspective on life or what is your mother/father like? Where did you grow up and what was your childhood like? Ask him about siblings and grandparents and if he has children ask him how often he sees them and what they're like. Ask what his long term self-development and professional or life goals are and ask him about his definition or vision of a healthy romantic relationship and whether or not he desires this and in what kind of time frame. Inquire about what he perceives to be his greatest personal as well as relationship strength and share yours. Ask him questions like what is the biggest mistake you made in a relationship and have you ever had a sexually transmitted disease? Include many or all of the following questions:

> What frustrates you?
> What is your philosophy of money?
> If you could change one thing about yourself, what would it be? Why?
> Why did your last relationship or marriage end and what was your role in it?
> Have you ever had a bisexual or homosexual experience?
> How would you describe your health?
> What is the biggest sacrifice your mom made for you?
> What's your relationship like with your dad?
> Where does your image of a man come from? Why?

What kind of activities do you enjoy doing with your children?

Chapter 11
His Network

As a sociologist, one of the most fascinating aspects of male-female relationships to me is social interaction. Some of those big qualifier questions can be answered or observable through what you witness within a man's social and family network. A man's network reveals his ability to maintain relationships and his reputation and offers the opportunity to gain important insights into his personal history. The network here encompasses his connection to family, friends and the community. Networks typically include people whom we trust and with whom have established relationships. Beware of dating a man for an extended period or committing to him unless you have investigated his network. I firmly believe if a man is interested in you that he will introduce you to his friends and family. If he doesn't, this may be a warning sign that he's not interested in you.

All relationships (family, friends, romantic, employment, church) have to be cultivated, nurtured and maintained to some degree. Someone has to initiate contact and the other person has to respond. The frequency of contact and the mode of communication may vary. He, like you, may speak to a parent or sibling every day and talk to good friends several times a week, month, or every few months. Dating has evolved in the information technology age, his interaction may be more through email, twitter, telephone, text, and Facebook, etc. What you really want to glean is the quality of his relationships and his behavior, attitude, and feelings about them. When evaluating your partner's network don't be concerned as much about the total number of family and friends that he interacts with but with the strength of the associations. Does he have strong or weak relationships with family and friends? Who does he lean on during good or difficult times and why? Who in his personal network exemplifies model social and ethical behavior? Who does he go to for career or relationship advice? Learn to appreciate and desire a partner with healthy family and friends and to pay attention when the opposite is true.

We all have disagreements and may have a difficult relationship with a parent, siblings, and/or a friend, so don't expect perfection. Look for the overall quality of those connections and consider how he responds to and deals with even those difficult relationships with close family. It is equally important to observe how he functions within your personal network. If you have strong, healthy family and friend relationships, his reactions and interactions to them and in turn their response to him are invaluable when you're trying to date and marry wisely.

I can't tell you how many times I've had a firm opinion about a boyfriend or someone close to me, but I didn't actually verbalize my thoughts. For instance, a close friend was dating a man that I didn't think was good for her. I really thought she deserved someone better. I observed that he was impatient with her and didn't seem respectful of her feelings. She behaved a bit timidly around him – a completely unnatural mode for my strong-natured, gregarious friend. I wanted to tell her so bad, but she never asked me for my opinion, and she liked him so much. In truth, I didn't want her to be angry at me because I felt our friendship was more important than my feelings. So I didn't say anything. Over time, she reached the same conclusions about him that I did, and they eventually broke up. Had she continued the relationship to the point, perhaps, of marriage and my concern continued to be validated, I hope that I would have had the courage to speak before she invested her future into a relationship with him. Established social and family networks provide not only a sense of belonging but a gauge for others to discover a lot more about you and for you to do the same. Remember Pastor Jeff? When I emerged into dating again after making progress addressing my pain over my father's distance in my life, I consulted with my father and several close friends when he made the "hang out at the hotel" proposition. My dad and friends affirmed what my initial instincts suggested: He was not the one! RUN!

I further understood the importance of networks when I dated Thomas. He was the one who wanted me to take out a $50,000 loan so he could open a retail store. He had just ended a long-term relationship and had relocated looking for a fresh start. While dating him, I eventually discovered that he had lived in multiple cities, moving every few years, and didn't have one relationship tie to his past. He didn't even keep in contact with his siblings, literally didn't know if they were alive or dead! About a year into our relationship, he woke up one morning and decided to move out west. Thomas's only reason was to get a fresh start on life. He was almost forty-five years old. He moved and abandoned me too. It shouldn't have taken his moving to end our relationship; I should have done that sooner. I had already discovered his broken family and social network and his propensity for cutting ties and moving on. I value my friends and family relationships. I learned to value this deeply about any man I dated as well. A man's substantial lack of quality commitments to family and friends is telling.

FAMILY WEB

Spending time with your man's family is a must. His past is relevant to the future because his childhood experiences may define his perspective of the world. Some of his past experiences may define who he is as a man and how he performs as a husband or father. Regardless of whether or not his childhood was functional or dysfunctional, you should want to know about it. His childhood family experience, just like yours, helped to shape his value system. The home environment is where learned behavior comes from whether it was negative and dysfunctional or healthy. If you're in a dating situation that seems headed for exclusivity or an engagement and your partner hasn't/doesn't take you around his family or discuss them, suspect that he's keeping something from you or that there's some dysfunction that should cause you concern. When you do go around his family, pay attention to what's said and the general tone and mood of his interactions with them and their attitudes and words towards him when he's not around. It's a serious red flag when a man's relationship with family and friends is a revolving door of short-term or broken relationships.

Dysfunctional family behavior is often passed down unless the cycle is confronted and resolved through therapy and alternative patterns of thinking, acting, and being. As I discussed early on in the book, it is absolutely essential to deal with your own family issues before trying to meet a man and starting a family of your own and it's just as essential that you know and weigh his family issues legacy, whether it's poor anger management, emotional and physical abuse, alcohol and/or drug abuse, molestation, incest, abandonment, mental instability, low self-esteem, infidelity, divorce, laziness, narcissism, pessimism, or immaturity, among a number of other things.

I shared the family issue that had the most impact on me. My grandmother Madelyn's parents divorced, and then she was abandoned by both her parents. My mother's parents divorced and then she was abandoned by her father. My parents divorced, and I was abandoned by my father. When I confronted my father and the history of divorce and single-mother parenting in my family, I emerged much more knowledgeable about myself, dad, and the impact of our family situation and prepared to make different decisions about my dating partners and potential husband. I've seen the impact of this issue in the relationships of some of the women I interviewed. One of them, Carla, found out about her husband's family issue only towards the end of their brief marriage and after the divorce. Her ex-husband, James, never had his father Patrick in his life. Patrick abandoned the family when James was a toddler. James could count on one hand how many times he saw his father over the course of his life. After their divorce, James disappeared on their two children. So far their children have not seen or heard from James in years.

Another woman, Sue, never knew that there was a family history of child molestation in her husband's family. He had shared the issues with drug and alcohol addiction but not the sexual abuse. Sue and Ken had two young children. Sue would allow members of Ken's family to babysit them. It wasn't until there was such an incident with one of the relatives that Sue found out about the history of molestation within the family. Sue and Ken's young daughter indicated that a male cousin had touched her inappropriately. When they confronted him, he confessed. They sought out professional help for their daughter and their family. During therapy, the counselor asked Sue about Ken's family dynamics, and this is how she found out. She learned more after contacting her sister-in-law who lived out of state and rarely visited or spoke to members of her own family. Tracy said that several generations of their family had been molested by various relatives and that's one of the many reasons she moved her family out of state so they wouldn't be influenced by family wounds.

Amanda was another woman who shared her story. She too married a man whose family history she knew little about. Her husband Luke grew up in a large family and didn't celebrate birthdays or holidays. Initially, she accepted it as a matter of his wanting to keep the true meaning of those important holidays in mind and not get caught up in the commercialism. It didn't bother her until they had children and attended his church more often. Most of the church members celebrated birthdays and holidays. Amanda and Luke argued over celebrating their children's birthdays and the holidays. Amanda wanted to celebrate the days she gave birth to them. On the other hand, Luke didn't believe it was a big deal. After all, growing up, no one celebrated his birthdays or the holidays and he turned out fine.

Amanda reached out to members of Luke's family and for the first time learned about his parents' alcoholism and drug addiction. They had often abandoned their children and gone on binges. Luke's parents never acknowledged their birthdays or holidays. So he grew up without such acknowledgement. He conformed to this and thought this behavior was acceptable for his children. It took a few years for Amanda to convince Luke that giving birth to her children was a blessing and among the best days of her life, and she wanted to celebrate with her children. Luke finally supported Amanda's beliefs. Now, they celebrate the children's birthdays and holidays.

Anyone can have a history of some kind of family dysfunction, but you can't afford to be ignorant about the history of the man in whom you're investing considerable time, emotional and social commitment, and affection and love. The issues that shaped his childhood could have him too warped, emotionally immature, and/or incompatible with your expectations and needs. If he's addressed those issues and is healing, and shares these honestly with you then he may still be a great partner choice for you, but don't close your eyes to this dynamic. Know that you need to be informed just as he should have vital information about the family issues that impacted you.

HIS MOTHER

A man's mother can be an incredible reference point for evaluating your partner. If she's alive and well, this is one of the many reasons that you should want to meet and spend time with her if you're getting serious in your relationship and before you become engaged or married. Most parents, especially moms, don't say negative things about their children, especially their sons. But if a mom does say something about her son then you should hang onto every word. A year or so after I graduated, I got together with a group of friends and associates from college. One of the women, in the group, Rachel, had been dating a man whose mother she felt was too possessive of him. Nick was in his mid-thirties and still living at home with his mother and working sporadically. Rachel went on to say that she recently had called Nick and his mother answered the telephone. When Rachel asked for

Nick, his mother said, "Honey, if you are dating my son, he means you no good. If I were you, I would run for the hills." Rachel was upset and believed Nick's mother was doing everything she could to keep them apart. I didn't know Rachel that well, so initially I didn't say a word.

Rachel continued complaining about his mother being in their business. Finally, I intervened and said, "Mothers usually don't say negative or harsh words about their sons. If I were you, I would take heed to every word she said about him." She ignored me. About two years later we got together again, and Rachel didn't come to the gathering. When we asked about her, we were told that Nick had moved in with Rachel and gotten her into a lot of debt. She lost her home and her job and had to file for bankruptcy. She was so embarrassed that she relocated to another city to start over. Nick returned to his mother's home. Rachel received critical information from the best source possible, Nick's mom, but she refused to listen.

A man's treatment of his mother, his interaction with her, and words about her also provide useful clues that indicate how he will treat the woman in his life. Is he bitter, angry or unforgiving or disrespectful to his mother? Or thoughtful and kind to his mother even if she wasn't a great mom to him? I recall my grandmother telling an aunt of mine, "Baby, if he don't treat his mama right, he sure won't treat you right." That's something I've never forgotten. Research has long suggested that the relationship between mother and child is not only critical but sets the tone for the rest of an individual's life. The mother-son relationship is a young man's first love experience with the opposite sex. This is the baseline by which men measure future relationships. According to John Bowlby (1951), a WHO Report, Maternal Care and Mental Health, "Mother love in infancy and childhood is as important for mental health as are vitamins and proteins for physical health."[59] I agree. Decades have passed since Bowlby reached his conclusions and increasing evidence supports his findings. You should want to see a bond between mother and son that isn't predicated on either's power over or control of the other. Does your partner acknowledge mom on special days such as birthdays and Mother's day? Spend some one-on-one time with his mom. Take her out to lunch or dinner and pay attention to her verbal and nonverbal cues.

---

[59] Bowlby, J. (1951). WHO Report *Maternal Care and Mental Health*. Geneva: World Health Organisation.

If your partner's mother is deceased you can still learn a lot about their relationship. How does your partner refer to her? Does your partner have fond memories of her? Does your partner share stories about her character? Does your partner mention her? Or, does your partner pretend she never existed? Unfortunately, my husband's mother passed before we even dated. I never met her. However, I can tell how my husband felt about his mother. He talks about her with such great fondness and laughter and he has positive reactions to his childhood memories. He loved and respected her and took care of her financially as she got older and her health declined.

HIS CHILDREN

If your partner has children from a previous relationship, pay attention to how he treats them as it is a terrible oversight not to do so, as Jackie found out. Even though the relationship didn't work out with the mother, he should be involved in every aspect of his child's life. Jackie, a woman I interviewed, dated Joe, a divorced man with one child. Jackie was with Joe on several occasions when his ex-wife Ann called regarding their child. She had recently lost her job and needed extra assistance for their daughter. It was wintertime in the upper Midwest where the temperature can drop below freezing. It was mid-November and Jane was begging her ex-husband to buy their young daughter a coat so she could stay warm while waiting for the school bus. Joe even admitted that Ann had never asked for additional support and did an excellent job with their daughter. He promised that he would get her a coat for a Christmas gift. In other words, his daughter would have to stay cold for several more weeks. Joe insisted that he didn't have additional money to help. However, he did manage to get money when he needed it for something he deemed important to him. Jackie ignored this big red flag.

    Jackie had been dating for almost a year when she became pregnant. Joe supported her decision to have the baby. Over the course of the pregnancy, they began to have relationship problems. Jackie wanted to be married and Joe didn't want to remarry. He wanted his freedom. Jackie had pregnancy complications and delivered their son prematurely. As soon as their son was born, they broke up and Joe started dating again. Jackie wasn't financially prepared to be off of work several months to care for their son. So she asked Joe for money to help with their child until she could return to work. She even provided him with a list of items the baby needed such as diapers for premature infants and special formula for infants with digestive issues and creams for his dry skin. He didn't buy one item for his child. Joe reminded Jackie about his daughter and his responsibilities to her. He said that he also needed money to live his life. Jackie had to rely on her family and the kindness of strangers for financial and emotional support. She had to hire a lawyer to establish paternity and obtain child support. She had been forewarned about Joe because she got a serious look at his behavior in regard to an important part of his family network – his own child.

FRIENDS

You don't have control over your biological family members. However, you do have free will to determine your network of friends and any man has that same empowerment. When I was in my early twenties, I met and fell in love with Cole. We broke up, but I wanted him back badly. So I decided to win him over. My emotions took over my mind. My plan was to go to his home and confront his new girlfriend and to tell her we were in love. If that didn't work, I was prepared for a fist fight. I explained this idea to my good friends. They talked me out of this crazy plan and are still my good friends today. I'm glad I didn't move forward because I would have made a fool of myself. Thank God for good friends.

    I remember my husband and I were married for about a year when we had our first big disagreement. I couldn't get him to understand my perspective and I couldn't see his point of view. I realized that we needed a mediator. I approached a couple, who were his good friends, for guidance. I hadn't known them for a really long time but my husband had and I had a lot of respect for them and their commitment to God and family. We met with them over several sessions, and they provided both of us with practical tools for negotiating our disagreement. Although we didn't change our minds, we were able to reach a mutual understanding. It could have been a mistake going to my husband's friends, but I had thoroughly examined his very strong network of friends before we married and found them to be overwhelmingly good, reasonable, Christian people who truly loved and supported my husband. They treated me with respect and made me feel welcomed during our social interaction, so I felt comfortable reaching out to people that I knew he would respond favorably to as well. They wanted us to resolve our problem amicably and had both of our best interests in mind. This is why his network of friendships, as is yours, is so important because you will need the support of others from time to time to get over a hurdle. It is critical your partner have a strong positive network of friends. You want to know who your partner has access to and who he will be getting advice from and if they reflect the values you admire in him and/or expect in a partner. You also want to check his ability to maintain positive intimate relationships.

HIS REPUTATION

Being plugged into the quality of a potential partner's social and family network also helps to reveal his reputation. Does he have good qualities such as humility, trustworthiness, and honesty? Do people communicate with him and include him in on discussions? Does he get invited to social events or family functions? Or do people avoid him? Remember Joseph whom I mentioned earlier. He didn't share my religious commitment and didn't respect it. He also felt superior to his siblings because he had a graduate degree, and they didn't have any formal education. He was angry at his parents for having a large family and raising them in poverty. He constantly criticized their lifestyles and low-paying jobs. Once, we decided to spend the weekend in his hometown which was a few hours away. Joseph hadn't been home in several months. I'll never forget his family. His mother asked what was he doing home. She didn't seem too excited to see him. I thought this was an odd reaction from a mom. His siblings didn't have much to say to him either. Whenever someone tried to talk to Joseph, he responded in a harsh negative tone. He got into a verbal altercation with one of his brothers. I had to calm him down. For the most part, I just sat and took it all in. I heard comments about Joseph like "We hate it when he comes home" and "I'm surprised you found a woman who can deal with your arrogant ass." Our weekend trip turned out to be a one-day visit. Joseph only had one friend, Lenny, and I had always questioned whether or not it was a genuine friendship. Joseph always had negative things to say to Lenny because he didn't finish college. Sometimes Lenny would avoid Joseph for days because he was tired of his condescending manner. Among his one friend and family members,

Joseph had a reputation for being selfish, arrogant, and contentious, and no one really liked him. His reputation was honestly earned.

YOUR NETWORK

As I've mentioned, your family and friend network can play an invaluable role in helping you to accurately discern whether or not a man may or may not be the right one to date and marry. First, you have to check the quality of your own network. Who offers you wise counsel and honest critique intended to support and help rather than harm? If you're missing that dad figure, what responsible, sensible male friends and relatives do you have that you can turn to with questions or advice about the behaviors or attributes of a man? Every woman who dates can use a good, honest, platonic male friend in her life that cares enough to tell her the truth if he sees something in the guy she's dating that's potentially harmful to her. This good male friend could be a former good guy boyfriend who remained your friend after your break-up, your brother, pastor, etc. Again, he should be someone who has your best interest in mind and is a proven friend, not a guy friend who has a romantic interest in you.

Invite your guy friend to interact with the man you're dating. Your friend is likely to be on the alert and pick up signs/clues which may signal potential problems that you need to consider. Maya, a good friend of mine, was dating one of the most eligible bachelors in the city, Alex. He was tall, dark, and handsome. His resume was impeccable too. He was an attorney with a very successful practice and financially well off. Maya dated him for a few months and enjoyed his company but realized something was missing. Every time she went out with him, she tried to convince herself to see him as a life-long partner but she couldn't. Something just didn't feel right to her but she didn't know what it was.

Maya introduced Alex to a good male friend of hers, Mike. Mike and Alex met at a social event. Afterwards, Mike shared his impressions with Maya. He said that while Alex was very kind and possessed a lot of expensive material items and was obviously well-traveled, none of his conversation referred to family, friends, and other things he enjoyed. All Alex discussed were his material possessions. Maya gained some clarity through Mike's observations. Alex had all the right surface stuff – some of which was important like his education and professional and financial stability, but lacked depth to his character. He was superficial. His life was focused too much on things and little on people and other aspects of life. Maya stopped dating him.

THE PAPERWORK

Once you're in a committed relationship and heading in the direction of marriage, I strongly recommend you sit down with your partner and be willing to exchange documentation that validates your personal history and current status (marital status, credit history, etc.) I know you may be cringing or withdrawing as you read this, but hang on and consider this important, too often neglected step. I can't tell you how many times I've heard a woman say she didn't want to ask her man for paperwork because she feared he would be offended and terminate the relationship. Some women are also afraid to ask for documents because they feel it shows a lack of trust. However, think about it like this. If you have a mature man who loves you, has your best intentions in mind, and wants to build a solid, honest foundation for your relationship then he will want to offer full disclosure and will want full disclosure from you. He may be uncomfortable about his less than perfect credit, but you both need to be adults and recognize that the first time you get an intimate peek into how your partner looks on paper should not be *after* you're married.

      Verifying his self-representation through observation is one part of it but verifying it through documentation is the other key part. Let's discuss how valuable documents are. Although my husband and I had been platonic friends for eighteen years, when the nature of our relationship changed so did my need to confirm more about him, including if my impression that he managed his finances well was correct. I was still a bit nervous about this step even though I had gotten committed to taking it with anyone I became serious about. It was lovely that now I could use my father as a sounding board about the documentation request step. He strongly supported that it was wise and a necessary part of our courtship since we were planning to marry. My husband-to-be and I had also agreed that he would be the breadwinner while we began a family. I needed to feel secure about his ability to take care of me and any children.

      His paperwork told a story as I combed through it. His will revealed his deep caring for his close family members, friends, home church, and community organizations. It reflected his core value system and confirmed what I had observed up to that point. Even though we attended college together and I called his office over the years, I still asked for copies of his undergraduate and graduate degrees. I even went through documents he forgot he had such as life insurance policies. His documents confirmed his salary, wise saving, and who he said he was, and I presented him with my pertinent documents as well. We also both underwent STD testing at the same time and exchanged our reports. There is no question that this should be something any woman should require if she's dating, sexually active, or planning to marry.

    I haven't always had a positive experience with this process. Remember Thomas, the 'entrepreneur' who asked me to take out a $50,000 business loan for him? Well, since he opened the door by asking me to sign for a small business loan, I asked to review his personal documents. Initially, he showed me documents such as his driver's license, birth certificate, and college degrees. He thought this would satisfy me, but it didn't. I wanted to see the financial documents. He kept giving me the run around and said that I should trust him. He declared that I would never get a man if this is what I required him to do. For weeks, he resisted. I didn't waver. He eventually provided the forms. I wasn't shocked by what was there. As a matter of fact, I expected it.

Thomas said he made about $70,000 a year, but when I looked at his check stub, his biweekly pay didn't add up to that amount. He only made about $45,000 a year. When I inquired about this discrepancy, he responded that he was anticipating a very generous bonus which he never received. His earnings were not a big issue for me, but his deception about it was. I also reviewed his credit report. It was a mess. He had joint accounts, with multiple women that were in default. I'm sure these other women were victims of his business deals. I learned that he rarely paid his bills within a reasonable time period and some bills he didn't pay at all. He was in default on his student loans. There was a state listed, which he'd never mentioned living in, showing debt with another woman. When I asked about that, Thomas told me about his wife, Charlotte. Well, he had never mentioned her before. Lastly, I reviewed his social security statement. There were years in which he had little or zero income. Now, at this point, Thomas was in his forties so this was disturbing. When I inquired about this issue,

Thomas said that he stayed at home for a few years and cared for the child of the woman with whom he was involved. After going through his paperwork, I had more questions than answers, and I lost all of the shaky respect that I had for him. His documents confirmed that he was not who he claimed to be.

Even though it can be uncomfortable to insist that this be a part of your transition from casual dating to serious commitment, you can't effectively prepare for marriage or a commitment where you merge lives and households without each of you having accurate portraits of how each of you conducts the daily business of life. Certainly, you don't want to be premature in requesting to see a man's documentation. This is not a step you take after you've merely gone out a couple of times; also, some information should be revealed earlier than others. A driver's license might be early on in the first several months but a will after you've decided to seriously commit to one another. Before you move in with someone or start planning that wedding, the following documentation should be on your mind to review:

- Birth certificate
- Payroll stub

- Benefits (Life Insurance, Health Insurance, Company Investments (401K, stock)
- Credit report from the three major agencies
- Taxes
- Driver's license
- Bank statements
- Criminal background report
- STD testing, including HIV TEST
- Diploma/degree
- Automobile registration and insurance
- Student loans
- Court records

Chapter 12
Moving Forward

If you have blamed yourself for your father's absence and been weighed down by low self-esteem and a strong sense of rejection and abandonment, you have surely felt the impact of it in your dating/love life. These feelings should be resolved before you pursue romantic relationships. The only way I know to heal from an absentee father is to get closure. This means taking a moment and conjuring up the past and acknowledging hurt and pain. Holding onto grudges binds us to our pain. This negative connection constantly reignites awful feelings and memories. This inadvertently gives your absentee father control over your life. Don't let this happen to you. Seek counseling to assist with this healing. Children take their immature childhood reasoning into their adult lives. The problem is that it will remain until it's addressed. Forgiveness is a crucial part of this healing. Forgiveness doesn't mean that you accept or excuse your father's behavior or absence. Forgiveness liberates you so that you can move forward with your life and pursue healthy love choices. One of the most powerful lessons that collecting information for this book affirmed for me is that our father's absence during childhood has absolutely nothing to do with us. If you've thus far had a traumatic dating life, fraught with poor choices and getting wounded, you can heal from this, become empowered, and learn to date in a more proactive, wise manner. I am living proof!

If your father is alive and approachable, as mine was, have a conversation with him. If your dad is deceased, unapproachable, or you don't know who he is, you can still bring your sorrow to an end. Write a letter to him. Tell him how his abandonment impaired your life and caused you low self-esteem, depression and any other damaging effects you've suffered. This is your moment to release your negative emotions. Prayer, mediation, counseling, support groups and self-help books are all tools to help you achieve this release. I couldn't reclaim all that I lost from growing up without a dad, the missed opportunities, the love and support, but even his absence provided a future opportunity to grow, learn, and become stronger. I was even blessed to be able to benefit from what he still could offer. Most importantly, once I let go of my daddy pain, I dated more healthily and eventually my husband came along.

SUMMARY

I've created a tool that I want to leave with you. It is a dating guide. As you uncover each aspect of your man's life, summarize your experience on this form and use it to analyze what you learn from it. Complete the first assessment generally by six-months. Please remember that dating is a process; you may not complete the section within this six-month frame but aim to do so. As your relationship evolves, you should have more information to add by the first-year evaluation. The first-year time frame, just like the six-month one, is just an estimate. Complete the guide at a steady pace. The goal is to use it to assist you in making sure that you thoroughly investigate all of the significant areas of his life. Finally, do be mindful that you will not find someone who has 100 percent of what you're looking for. Everyone has some weaknesses, but you need not accept the problematic attributes and dysfunction that I've outlined in this book as normal!

The overall goal is to make sure that you can make rational decisions about what constitutes quality in a man and that you're not dating in the darkness, unaware of how your unresolved girlhood issues might blind you to details about a man that you should take seriously.

You want to be able to accurately discern his social and internal character, strengths and weaknesses, and determine his fitness and suitability as a date and partner. Dating can actually be fun and rewarding, but it requires common sense and strategic skills. Claim your right to healthy dating and healthy relationships! You're worth safeguarding! Happy dating!

DATING GUIDE
6 Month Review
(In each category write the term positive or negative and record specific examples in the notes section)

	Words	**Behavior**
His mind		
His ability to love		
How he manages his emotions		
Manage finances		
Relationships to others		
His wisdom		
How he functions socially		
How he thinks of others		
His gratification		
How understanding of cause of effect		
His network (family & friends)		
His family		
Family history and issues		
Mother–Son relationship		
Mother cues		

His friends

His children

His reputation

His religion

His communication style

His interrogation

His paperwork

DATING GUIDE
1 Year Review
(In each category write the term positive or negative and record specific examples in the notes section)

	Words	Behavior
His mind		
His ability to love		
How he manages his emotions		
Manage finances		
Relationships to others		
His wisdom		
How he functions socially		
How he thinks of others		
His gratification		
How understanding of cause of effect		
His network (family & friends)		
His family		
Family history and issues		
Mother–Son relationship		
Mother cues		

His friends

His children

His reputation

His religion

His communication style

His interrogation

His paperwork

DATING NOTES

DATING NOTES

DATING NOTES

Made in the USA
Charleston, SC
18 June 2015